i

Metamorphosis

75 Years History of District 8

Author: Farzana Chohan
Editor: Eileen Murphy
Historian: Gary White

DEDICATION

Members of District 8
From 1940 to 2016

Table of Contents

DEDICATION V

ACKNOWLEDGMENTS IX

INTRODUCTION XI

1 THE FORMATION OF DISTRICT 8..1

2 TIMELINE OF DISTRICT 8...7
    75 YEARS AND BEYOND! 82

3 CHRONICLE OF DISTRICT 8 CONFERENCES..83

4 NOTEWORTHY...123

5 LIFELONG UNDERTAKINGS...129

6 DISTRICT 8: HALL OF FAME 143

7 PICTOGRAPH...151

8 NOTES..167
    NOTE FROM FARZANA CHOHAN 169
    NOTE ABOUT GARY WHITE..171
    NOTE FROM EILEEN MURPHY 172
    ACRONYMS 174

ACKNOWLEDGMENTS

I would like to acknowledge Gary White, Historian of District, who has done an incredible job in maintaining the 75-year history of district, both in terms of documentation and artifacts.

Past District Governor Gary and his wife Sherry White (also a Past District Governor from Chicago) have allocated a substantial part of their house to accumulate historical information for many years. They have done exhibits at conferences, which have provided members of District glimpses into the historical journey of District 8 since 1940.

As such I would like to acknowledge Gary White for his tremendous work.

And, Sherry, without your support to Gary and District, it would not have been possible to keep it together!

I want to acknowledge Elizabeth Link and Mary Kerwin for their assistance on the project.

I would like to acknowledge Eileen Murphy. She worked as editor of this book. It was Eileen Murphy's enthusiasm, her spirit and her tireless work on this document that made it possible to wrap up the work, which was started over four years ago!

There are countless more who have assisted in making this book a reality.

Thank you all for your spirit of friendship!

INTRODUCTION

Toastmasters International traces its roots all the way back to 1905, when its founder-to-be, Ralph Smedley, began conducting informal public speaking programs during his time working at the YMCA in Bloomington, Illinois.

Smedley eventually moved to California and continued to follow his passion to foster public speaking skills at YMCA facilities there. Utilizing speech and operating manuals produced by Smedley himself, his fledgling program took root and quickly flourished as its methods proved themselves to be effective in developing speaking and leadership skills. The Toastmasters International organization we know today was officially incorporated as a non-profit organization in 1932.

Today, Toastmasters International is comprised of approximately 15,900 clubs operating in 142 countries. The program supports more than 345,000 members worldwide. The organization is divided into fourteen geographic regions, including North America, Europe, Australia, Southeast Asia, the Pacific Islands, and parts of South America and Africa. Each region is divided further into districts, which can range in size from one or two states in the U.S. to entire countries in other parts of the world depending on the number of clubs in a given location.

District 8 currently incorporates eastern Missouri and southwestern Illinois, with the city of St. Louis as the center of the district (both geographically and in terms of club density).

1

THE FORMATION OF DISTRICT 8

1. THE FORMATION OF DISTRICT 8

Gary White, DTM, PDG

District 8 Historian

District 8 has a long and distinguished history in Toastmasters. Toastmasters was developing rapidly in California in the late 1930s; however, the heartland of America did not yet have any districts. A geographical region needed at least 10 clubs to form a district. When the states of Illinois and most of Missouri reached that level in 1940, the Toastmasters International Board of Directors approved the formation of District 8, just before more pressing matters occupied the country.

The first District Governor was Robert W. Williamson of Springfield, IL, who served until August of 1941. Toastmasters International created the Basic manual in 1942. WWII affected the District in many ways, but the most notable was that Clinton Sandusky, District Governor in 1943-44, was inducted into military service and the term was completed by Bert Mann. The district had 260 members in 1944, the mileage allowance was 2c per mile, and the hotel expense was $3.00 for delegates. This large geographical region worked together, but it was a challenge. Dr. Ralph Smedley, founder of Toastmasters, visited the Urbana-Champaign Area in 1946 (now part of District 54). Also in 1946, District Governor Bertram Mann expressed a desire to have a directory of club meeting dates, places, and contacts that became the forerunner of the Resource Manual. By 1947, the District had 515 members and the clubs were grouped into eight areas, which included St. Louis and Chicago as the focal points.

There was an informal agreement that the District Governor would switch between the Chicago and St. Louis locations at each election. By April 1949, the District had grown to 1100 members. District Governor Russell Puzey established a goal to split the district, which he achieved by the end of his term on 1 July 1950. District 8 maintained Missouri and Illinois south of Chicago. District 30 was formed in Northern Illinois close to Chicago.

The split was approved at the 1949 18th International Convention of Toastmasters, which was held in St. Louis, MO. The International organization had also been growing, and there were now 750 Toastmaster Clubs in 41 States, as well as Canada and Scotland. This convention was well received, and Dr. Smedley was even quoted as saying, "That meeting went into our history as one of the most useful and helpful Conventions we have ever held." District 8 continued to grow. In 1956, District 54 was created in central Illinois. It was enlarged in 1964, 1971, and 1976, all from Counties in District 8, which moved the D8 boundary further south each time.

The 32nd Annual Convention of Toastmasters International was also held in St. Louis, MO in 1963. At that time, there were 3,600 Clubs scattered all over the world, except behind the Iron Curtain. The semi-annual duess were $6.00, just raised from $4.50. District 8 had 53 clubs and 1137 members. In 1968, club officer terms changed from 01Apr.- 01Oct. to 01Jan-01Jul.

District 8 was at a low of 43 clubs in 1973. International Bylaws were changed to admit women to membership in August 1973. The most recent Annual Toastmaster International Convention to be held in St. Louis was on 21-24 August 1996 at the Adam's Mark Hotel.

Many of Toastmasters International's leaders have been selected from District 8.

Three International Presidents from District 8

Russell Puzey
Aubrey Hamilton
Earl Potter

Five International Directors from District 8

Bertram Mann (1946-47),
Harry Hodde (1952-53),
Adam Bock (1966-67),
Ted Randall (1985-86),
Charlie Rogers (1989-1991),
Floy Westermeier (1998-2000),
Chuck Carpenter (2001-2003)

The District leadership originally consisted of the District Governor, Lt. Gov. for Education, and the two Division Lt. Governors (Missouri and Illinois Divisions). At the 1968 Spring Conference, the position of Lt. Governor for Administration was created. As the number of clubs grew, the Divisions were increased to four (MO. South, Mo. No., Il. No. and Il. So. Divisions). Then, in 1983, the number of Divisions was increased to six and more descriptive names were developed (MO. South, Three Rivers, Prairie, Great Rivers, Mo. West, and Gateway Divisions). Toastmasters International entered the computer world at this same time, and the Divisions were given single letter designations (A-F) to be more compatible with the new computers.

4

District 8 has been listed in the Toastmasters' Hall of Fame as a Distinguished District as follows:

President's Distinguished District

1982-83 Harry Pleis, ATM District Governor

Select Distinguished District

1995-96 Floy Westermeier, DTM District Governor

2009-10 Dori Drummond, DTM District Governor

2015-16 Farzana Chohan, DTM District Director

Distinguished District

1969-70 Wilbur J. Fox District Governor

1976-77 Virgil Greene District Governor

1978-79 Ed Richfield District Governor

1979-80 Ted Randall District Governor

1983-84 Paul Lloyd, ATM District Governor

1985-86 Gary White, DTM District Governor

1986-87 Charlie Rogers, DTM District Governor

1987-88 Al Ott, DTM District Governor

1988-89 George Peo, DTM District Governor

1990-91 Lorraine Newgent, DTM District Governor

1992-93 Chuck Carpenter, DTM District Governor

1993-94 Ted Wear, DTM District Governor

1997-98 Jean Inabinett, DTM District Governor

1999-2000 Carole Breckner, DTM District Governor

2007-08 Barbara Kryvko, DTM District Governor

2008-09 Tony Gartner, DTM District Governor

2010-11 Tim Spezia, DTM District Governor

Presidential Citations from Toastmasters International for Distinguished Service to Toastmasters of District 8

1977 Wilfrid B. Finuf, DTM

1987 Wilbur J. Fox, DTM

1989 C. C. McBrian

1992 Tom Houston, ATM

1992 Ted Randall, DTM

1993 Dick Weber, DTM

2000 Lora Mae Stewart

2003 Dr. Steve Watson, DTM

2

TIMELINE OF DISTRICT 8

District Governors:

1940 – 1941 Robert Williamson, Springfield, IL

1941 – 1942 Wesley Olson, Quincy, IL

1943 – 1944 Clinton Sandusky, Danville, IL; Bertram Mann

Battle Born

December, 1940

The Toastmasters International Board of Directors officially incorporates District 8, comprising all of Missouri and Illinois. The Lincoln Douglas Club (51), chartered in 1936, is one of the founding members. Robert Williamson of Springfield, IL is chosen as Governor of the fledgling District.

February, 1941

The February, 1941 issue of Toastmaster Magazine, dedicated to the life of President Abraham Lincoln, features photographs from the Lincoln Douglas Club in Illinois. The issue also covers a debate between the St. Louis Toastmasters Club and the Washington University Debate team on the topic: "Resolved, Power of the Federal Government Should be Increased."

Wesley Olson (pictured) of Quincy, IL becomes District Governor.

> December 7, 1941: The Japanese attack Pearl Harbor, Hawaii, drawing the United States into World War II.

1943

Clinton Sandusky of Danville, IL becomes District Governor. He is soon conscripted into military service, and his term is finished by Bertram Mann.

District Governors:
1944 – 1945 Alvin Otto, Jacksonville, IL
1945 – 1946 Wilbert Metzger, Alton, IL

1944

Midtown Club (283) is chartered in Clayton, MO. District membership reaches 260. The District provides dignitaries travel allowances of 2¢ per mile on gas and $3.00 on hotel room accommodations. Still, the large area of the District creates difficulties in bringing Toastmasters from different locations together.

> June, 1944:
> Allied forces invade the beaches of Normandy in France, beginning the liberation of Western Europe after years of occupation. Germany surrenders eleven months later, ending the war in Europe.

1945

Alvin Otto of Jacksonville, IL becomes District Governor. He is succeeded by Wilbert Metzger of Alton, IL.

> August, 1945:
> President Harry Truman orders atomic bombs to be dropped on the Japanese cities of Nagasaki and Hiroshima. Within days of this display of destructive power, Japan surrenders, bringing World War II to an end.
>
> The United States recovers quickly and begins a period of economic and social growth that shapes the country for decades to come.

District Governors:
1946 – 1947 Bertram Mann, Jr., PID, St. Louis, MO
1947 – 1948 Norman Higgs, Chicago, IL

Building a Foundation

1946

Dr. Ralph Smedley (pictured), founder of Toastmasters, visits the Urbana-Champaign Area of District 8. The District also includes Smedley's hometown of Waverly, IL and the site of the first preliminary Toastmasters Club - Bloomington, IL.

1947

District Governor Bertram Mann suggests that a directory of club meeting dates, locations, and contacts be made. The idea leads to the creation of the Toastmasters Resource Manual.

District membership reaches 515. Clubs are grouped into 8 areas across the two states, mainly in St. Louis and Chicago. To alleviate logistical problems with managing such a large District, an unofficial rule is made that candidates from these two areas will take turns at each election for District Governor.

Norman Higgs of Chicago, IL becomes District Governor. Webster Groves Club (461) is incorporated in Webster Groves, MO; St. Clair Toastmasters Club (496) in Belleville,

April, 1947:

Jackie Robinson becomes the first African-American player in Major League Baseball. That season, the World Series is broadcast live on television for the first time.

IL; Capital Toastmasters (503) in Jefferson City, MO; Tarsus Toastmasters (532) in St. Louis, MO.

District Governors:

1948 – 1949 William Beukema, St. Louis, MO

1949 – 1950 Russell Puzey, Chicago, IL

Life magazine publishes an article about Toastmasters.

1948

William Beukema of St. Louis, MO becomes District Governor.

DIRECTOR: **WILLIAM J. BEUKEMA**   District 8

1204 North 8th Street, St. Louis 6, Missouri.
Club: St. Louis 170, St. Louis, Missouri.
Served: Area Governor; District Lieutenant Governor: District Governor; TI Convention and Club of the Year Committees. Member for 7 years, and has attended 4 TI Conventions.
Occupation: Chief Bookkeeper — Municipal Department.

1949

Members of St. Louis Toastmasters Club create a Missouri Good Roads Campaign speakers bureau. Future District Governor Aubrey Hamilton serves as chairperson.

District Lt. Governor Emmit Holmes presents an award to Dr. Gene Osello of Roseland Toastmasters Club in Chicago for greatest improvement in speech and greatest service to the club.

> 1948-1949:
>
> The still-occupied former country of Germany is officially divided into two territories: East Germany, controlled by the Soviet Union, and West Germany, under the supervision of the former Allied nations.

Wilson Ave Club in Chicago hosts a constitutional convention program in advance of the Illinois Constitutional Convention scheduled for the following year. Incoming District Governor Russell Puzey calls it, "Very interesting."

Kirkwood Club wins the District 8 Club-of-the-Year Award. Past President Robert Rosenheim presents the award to current President William Spain. Wilson Ave Club receives an honorable mention.

Russell Puzey of Chicago, IL becomes District Governor. He announces a goal to split the oversized district in half, establishing District 30 in Chicago and the surrounding areas.

District 8—**RUSSELL V. PUZEY**, Chicago, Governor. An Illinoisan, resident of Chicago since 1936. Graduate of University of Illinois; a Certified Public Accountant, partner in accounting firm of Frazer and Torbet. Member of Wilson Avenue Toastmasters Club, No. 169, since 1945; past Area Governor and District Secretary. First objective as Governor: to divide Dist. 8 into two well-organized districts. Second: to advance Toastmasters work in Chicago and vicinity. Motto: "For advancement, be a Toastmaster."

August, 1949

The 18th annual Toastmasters International Convention is held in St. Louis. Advertisements highlight the city's central location in the United States to encourage members from all over the country to attend. Puzey's goal of dividing District 8 comes to fruition, and he is elected to the International Board of Directors. The Convention is an outstanding success, with founder Ralph Smedley noting that it, "... went into our history as one of the most useful and helpful Conventions we have ever held." The planning committee is featured on the back cover of the Toastmaster magazine.

Toastmasters Leonard Schwartz of Edwardsville and F.G. Elliott of Midtown are appointed Illinois Director of Conservation and Vice President of the Indiana Limestone Company, respectively.

District Governors:

1950 – 1951 George Boardman Perry, Webster Groves, MO

1950

George Boardman Perry of Webster Groves, MO becomes District Governor. The split between District 8 and the newly-formed District 30 goes into effect. A new directory of clubs in District 8 is published:

Alton (230) – Selheim's Rest

*St. Clair (496) – Belleville, IL, Amlung's Cafe

McKinley (467) – Champaign YMCA

Commodore (654) – Decatur, The Surrey

Edwardsville (589) – Edwardsville Café

Mt. Vernon (882) – L&N Café

Downtown (538) – Quincy, IL, Am. Legion

Clayton (880) – Vernon's Cafeteria

*Capital (503) – Jefferson City, Florence's Café

KaCee (742) – Kirkwood, El Avion

Logan College (820) – Normandy Cafeteria

St. Louis (170) – Downtown YMCA

*Midtown (283) – St. Louis, Melbourne Hotel

Metropolitan (348) – St. Louis, Mark Twain Hotel

Bert Mann (802) – St. Louis, North Side YMCA

Illini (282) – Alton, IL, Skagg's

Bloomington (850) – Servrite Steak House

Bi-County (826) – Columbia, IL, Sangralle

East St. Louis (845) – Bush's Steak House

Athenian (174) – Jacksonville, IL, Hotel Dunlap

Quincy (129) – The Plaza

*Lincoln-Douglas (51) – Springfield, IL YMCA

Ferguson (525) – Ferguson Country Club

Kirkwood (594) – Ed Biase's

Piasa (661) – Maplewood, The Tulip Box

Overland (583) – Guy Miller's Cafeteria

Tyro (194) – St. Louis, North Side YMCA

Carondelet (286) – St. Louis, Carondelet YMCA

*Tarsus (532) – St. Louis, Little Bevo Rest

*Webster Groves (461) – YMCA

Algonquin (662) – Webster Groves, Yan Horn's Farm

* = Clubs still active today, more than 65 years after this list was printed.

14

District Governors:
1951 – 1952 Aubrey Hamilton, PIP, St. Louis, MO

1951-1952

Joseph Kassly, past president of East St. Louis Toastmasters and Deputy Governor of District 8, is presented the East St. Louis Jr Chamber of Commerce Distinguished Service Award.

October, 1951:
I Love Lucy
premiers on
television.

Toastmasters International president George Reed writes about the differences between "Democracy vs Communism" and the dangers of Communism. The Staff writes a 2-page special on "Milepost to Peace and Security, 1215, 1776, 1945" and encourages the growth of the United Nations.

Aubrey Hamilton of St. Louis, MO becomes District Governor.

District 8—AUBREY B. HAMILTON, St. Louis, Missouri, Governor. Attorney; Associate City Counselor, City of St. Louis; City Attorney for Hazelwood and Moline Acres. Former member of Missouri Legislature and Missouri Committee on Legislative Research. Charter member of St. Louis Club No. 170; past officer of club, area; Lt. Gov. 1950. Ambitions: "To emphasize educational service to clubs, formation of new clubs, and encouragement of community service by clubs and individual Toastmasters."

The District 8 map (pictured below as part of a promotion for the 1952 Toastmasters International Convention), shrinking consistently over the past few years, encompasses all of Missouri except the far western edge (near Kansas City and Joplin) and the southern part of Illinois. Lawrence Green represents District 8 in the International

TREASURER: **BERTRAM H. MANN, JR.**   District 8

Club: Tyro 194, St. Louis, Missouri.

Served: Area Governor; Dist. Governor; Director. Member Convention Local Activities (Chairman); By-Laws Com.; Rezoning and Elections Study Committee. Member 11 years.

Occupation: Patent Lawyer.

Speech Contest.

15

District Map - 1952

21st ANNUAL Convention
PALMER HOUSE
CHICAGO
AUG. -14-16

TOASTMASTERS INTERNATIONAL

Expansion in Illinois

—Photo by Dave Knoebel

Collinsville is a city of 12,000 population, located 10 miles east of East St. Louis. It is the center of a coal-mining region, and is close to the famous Cahokia Indian Mounds, a scenic attraction which many may visit enroute to the Chicago Convention.

The new Toastmasters Club at Collinsville was chartered recently at an impressive ceremony, attended by Mayor Louis Jackstadt and other local notables, together with a crowd of local and visiting Toastmasters. District Governor Aubrey Hamilton, of St. Louis, is seen in the picture, presenting the charter to Club President Elmer Pintar. The new club meets on Tuesday evenings, at the Fairmont Hotel.

Pictures from the spring and summer month issues of *Toastmaster* magazine feature District 8:

They Met in East St. Louis

Here are some of the leaders of District 8, who met in East St. Louis to plan activities for 1952. They appear thus in the picture: Al Brainerd, dep. gov. of East St. Louis Club; Harry Hodde, of Springfield, Illinois, lieut. gov.; Phil Ogden, of East St. Louis, area governor; R. H. Rosenthal, of Edwardsville, and Dale Fink of Wood River, each a deputy governor.

The Speech Contestants

This is the way they lined up, before the contest program got under way and the welkin began to ring. Hugh McEvoy, seated at the left, was the Speech Contest Chairman. Paul Brasch, at the extreme right, was the toastmaster for the contest. The speakers, from left to right, are Richard S. Wilson, Kenneth L. Teegarden, Ree Montgomery, G. Willard Bassett, Lawrence Green, and George W. Armstrong.

District Governors:

1952 – 1953 Harry Hodde, Springfield, IL

1953 – 1954 Phillip H. Ogden, East St. Louis, IL

1954 – 1955 Godfrey G. Harnett, Webster Groves, MO

1952 – 1953

D—8
H. L. HODDE

Harry L. Hodde of Springfield, IL becomes District Governor.

The Lincoln-Douglas Club raises funds for a recording machine to allow members to listen to their own speeches and give self-feedback. This is noted in the article "What's Going On" in the August 1952 issue of Toastmaster magazine.

Past District 8 Governor George Boardman Perry writes "Practice Every Day," encouraging Toastmasters to develop their diction, gestures, voice, sincerity, and enthusiasm to improve their speeches.

1953 – 1954

Phillip H. Ogden of East St. Louis, IL becomes District Governor.

1954 – 1955

Godfrey G. Harnett of Webster Groves, MO becomes District Governor.

> January, 1953:
>
> Famed WWII General Dwight David Eisenhower is inaugurated as President of the United States.

> 1953:
>
> The St. Louis Cardinals are set to move to Houston, Texas, until the team is purchased by the Anheuser-Busch brewery company.

District Governors:

1955 – 1956 Joe Tragesser, East St. Louis, IL

1956 – 1957 Paul Gnadt, St. Louis, MO

1957 – 1958 Arnold Denkert, Springfield, IL

1955 – 1956

Joe Tragesser of East St. Louis, IL becomes District Governor.

Toastmasters International publishes an updated Basic Training for Toastmasters, a manual written by founder Ralph Smedley, to guide members through the basics of mastering public speaking. In a note at the beginning of the book, Smedley himself describes the manual as, "an introduction to public speaking, designed to help you progress systematically toward your greater personal development through the laboratory which is your Toastmasters club."

D—8
J. G. TRAGESSER

1956 – 1957

Paul Gnadt of St. Louis, MO becomes District Governor.

1957 – 1958

Arnold Denkert of Springfield, IL becomes District Governor.

8—Paul Gnadt

1957:

The Soviet Union successfully launches humanity's first artificial satellite, named Sputnik. The momentous scientific achievement is a great concern to the United States government.

8—Arnold Denkert

District Governors:

1958 – 1959 George Brown, Creve Coeur, MO

1959 – 1960 Guy Thompson, Decatur, IL

Race for the Future

1958 – 1959

George Brown becomes District Governor. Past District 8 Governor Harry Hodde becomes one of two Regional Directors for Region V. The international leadership is being restructured to represent specific zones.

Ethan Shepley, Chairman of Washington University in St. Louis, is elected president of the board of directors for the newly-formed Toastmasters International Foundation.

John Argo, a Boy Scout from Overland, MO, becomes the first person to participate in joint programs between the Boy Scouts and Toastmasters. Hannibal, MO is selected as "Toastmaster Town of the Month" in 1959.

Toastmasters founder Ralph Smedley urges all Toastmasters to be educated about the spread of Communism and recommends the book *Masters of Deceit*, by J. Edgar Hoover.

1959 – 1960: Guy Thompson becomes District Governor. Past District 8 Governor Aubrey Hamilton, now International President of Toastmasters, presents his Year in Review. It is publicized in the August, 1959 issue of *Toastmaster* magazine.

8—Guy G. Thompson

The Golden Gavel award, now the highest honor bestowed by Toastmasters International to recognize "an individual distinguished in the fields of communication and leadership," is bestowed for the first time to Dr. Frank Baxter, a television personality and Professor Emeritus at the University of Southern California.

Scott Officers Club and East St. Louis Toastmasters hold "Whoppers Night" contest. Distinguished guests include: Guy Thompson, Malcolm MeLain, Earl Potter, and Col.Robert Engle, TI Consultant for Military Clubs.

July, 1958: The National Aeronautics and Space Administration is founded, the U.S.'s first step in the "Space Race."

District Governors:

1960 – 1961 Carlos Harrison, Kirkwood, MO

1961 – 1962 Earl Potter, PIP, Belleville, IL

1960 – 1961

Carlos Harrison becomes District Governor. O'Fallon Toastmasters Club (994) is incorporated in O'Fallon, IL.

The Scott NCO (Non-commissioned officer) Club is incorporated at Scott Air Force Base in southern Illinois. The ceremony includes honoring a "Four Chaplains" winner. The annual Fun Frolic, held by the Scott Officers Club, the new Scott NCO Club and five others, draws over 3oo Toastmasters and guests.

1961 – 1962

Earl Potter of Belleville, IL becomes District Governor.

The Lincoln-Douglas Club holds a special Past Presidents Night, with fifteen of the club's former presidents in attendance: Louis Keinzler, George Myers, Ted Ebel, Truman Dasher, Jerry Marrin, Jim North, Hershel Cudsworth, Solon Marr, Sam Buddemeier, Jack Glas, Arnold Denkert, John Dial, Harry Hodde, Charles McBrian, and Robert Bird.

8—Earl M. Potter
Belleville, Ill.

McDonnell Aircraft Club notes that they have coordinated with the McDonnell Speakers Bureau to present over fifty public speeches, mostly dealing with Project Mercury – the codename of the first human spaceflight program in the United States.

Plus Factor club presents public speeches in support of the Mayor's Pedestrian Traffic Safety Campaign. The number of injuries and deaths from pedestrian-involved motor vehicle accidents decreases.

> February, 1962:
>
> John Glenn becomes the first American astronaut to orbit the Earth.

District Governors:

1962 – 1963 Jerome Marrin, Springfield, IL

1963 – 1964 Malcolm McLean, East St. Louis, IL

1962 – 1963

B—J. R. Marrin
Springfield, Ill.

Jerome R. Marrin of Springfield, IL becomes District Governor.

Past District 8 Governor Earl Potter is selected as a Region V Director.

Richard Oglesby of the Lincoln-Douglas Club publishes "Founded Upon a Rock" in the June, 1963 issue of *Toastmaster* magazine. The article stresses the importance of good evaluation, both to individual speeches and to the club as General Evaluator.

October, 1962: A U-2 flying a recon mission over Cuba discovers Soviet missile deployments. It is shot down, and President John F. Kennedy responds with a naval blockade. The incident, known as the Cuban Missile Crisis, is resolved peacefully.

St. Clair and Plus Factor Clubs conduct a joint meeting.

Ellis Arnold of the Commodore Club is elected mayor of Decatur, IL. His campaign manager is Past District Governor Guy Thompson.

St. Louis again hosts the TI Convention, featuring a moonlight cruise and dinner dance, among other events. The full conference registration is $6.

TI proposes a $3 increase in duess, from $7 per year to $10 per year.

1963 – 1964

Malcolm McLean becomes District Governor. TI proposes several policy changes. The most significant is the change in age requirement from 21 to 18, meant to allow all military servicemen to join.

St. Clair Club places number 1 in the Top-10 Clubs. East St. Louis also makes the list.

District Governors:

1964 – 1965 Leo Seiffert, Cape Girardeau, MO

1965 – 1966 Junior Edwards, Belleville, IL

1964 – 1965

Leo Seiffert of Cape Girardeau, MO becomes District Governor. Toastmasters International announces a Toastmasters Day at the World's Fair following the annual convention.

8—Leo F. Seiffert
Cape Girardeau, Mo.

> **Ralph Smedley kicks off the celebration of the 40th Anniversary of Toastmasters with the following messages:**
>
> **Keep it Simple**
>
> **Do It Yourself**
>
> **Belief in the Individual**
>
> **Learn in Moments of Enjoyment**

July, 1964: The Civil Rights Act of 1964 prohibits discrimination based on race, color, religion, sex, or national origin, elevating minorities, immigrants, and women from their legal standing as second-class citizens.

Allen Brandt from Bridgeton represents District 8 in the Region-level International Speech Contest.

Past District Governor Earl Potter receives the District 8 Toastmaster of the Year award.

1965 – 1966

Junior Edwards becomes District Governor.

In July of 1965, Dr. Ralph Smedley, founder of Toastmasters International, passes away at the age of 87. The November issue of *Toastmaster* magazine is dedicated to his memory.

The University of Missouri Gavel Club receives its Certificate of Affiliation. Past District 8 Governor Earl Potter from the St. Clair Club is represented on the TI candidates page in his running for Vice President Education. The first Toastmasters Youth Leadership class graduates. St. Clair and East St. Louis Clubs both place in the Top-10 Clubs list.

September, 1966: *Star Trek* premieres on television.

District Governors:

1966 – 1967 Adam Bock, Lincoln, IL

1966 – 1967

8—Adam F. Bock
Lincoln, Ill.

Adam Bock of Lincoln, IL becomes District Governor. Fort Leonard Wood Club (493) is incorporated in Missouri. Webster Groves, Ferguson, and St. Clair Clubs celebrate their 20th anniversaries.

The Governor of Missouri is pictured with Adam Bock, Ken Miller, and Peter Scott proclaiming a Toastmasters Month. Charles Holsheiser receives a service award from District Governor Adam Bock.

Earl Potter is successfully elected International Vice President Education. He publishes "Improve Yourself, Use the Manuals" in the March, 1967 issue of *Toastmaster* magazine. He is quickly nominated for Senior Vice President.

The International Board of Directors sets a requirement for clubs to maintain a minimum of seven members.

January, 1967: Super Bowl I is played in the Coliseum in Los Angeles, CA. The Green Bay Packers defeat the Kansas City Chiefs 35-10.

District Governor:

1967 – 1968 Ken Miller, St. Louis, MO

1967 – 1968

8—Ken Miller
St. Louis, Mo.

Ken Miller of St. Louis, MO becomes District Governor.

Centralia Club is featured in an article about Speechcraft. Overland, St. Clair, and Carlinville Clubs are cited for outstanding membership gains. Webster Groves Club receives an honorable mention for its participation in a membership drive contest. The club gained 13 new members.

The August, 1967 issue of *Toastmaster* magazine features a two-page spread of District 8's homage to the late Dr. Ralph Smedley. Six photographs with captions show the dedication of the Waverly Memorial in Smedley's hometown in Illinois. A revised edition of Smedley's Basic Manual becomes available.

Earl Potter is elected Senior Vice President. He is later nominated for International President. St. Clair Club is again recognized as a Top-10 Club.

William Carroll, former president of Winged Words Club, is appointed postmaster of Hazelwood, MO. The club also makes Maj. Gen. John Norton, commander of the U.S. Army Aviation Material Command, an honorary member.

The Board of Directors recommends increasing duess to $12 per year.

April, 1968: Reverend Martin Luther King, Jr., a prominent leader of the Civil Rights Movement, is assassinated. His renowned "I Have a Dream" speech is considered to be among the greatest pieces of oratory in American history.

Members of Pana Club act as masters-of-ceremony at the Tri-County annual fair.

District Governors:

1968 – 1969 Robert Downing, Beason, IL

1968 – 1969

Robert Downing of Beason, IL becomes District Governor. Clayton Club celebrates its 20th anniversary. St. Louis is Toastmasters Town of the Month.

The Board of Directors publishes a new organizational chart with the districts organized into eight international regions. They also develop guidelines for speaking and coordinating outside the club.

8—Robert E.
Downing
Beason, Ill.

Missouri Congressman Thomas Curtis recognizes District Lt. Governor Earl Drennen for his club service and pledges support for Toastmasters.

Olney Club is cited for gaining nine new members and Jefferson County Club for seven. Taxtoasters is listed as a "Full" club with a membership of 40.

Thursday Noon Club works with the League of Women Voters to organize a speakers bureau. Lincoln Trails club presents a program to the Sullivan, IL Kiwanis Club.

St. Clair Toastmasters again places in the Top-10 Clubs.

Earl Potter becomes International President. The September, 1968 issue of *Toastmaster* magazine prints a two-page spread with biographical information about Potter, as well as his presidential address focusing on "Clubs on the Move Serve and Grow." The December issue shows a picture of Potter with the Noonday Club and his own St. Clair Club.

A later issue covers his national tour, including photos from El Paso, TX (District 23); with the Moorhead mayor (D20); with the Sacramento mayor (D39); visits in Districts 64, 16, 3, 14, and 42; and a picture of Potter with future U.S. President Ronald Reagan in District 39. The article also recounts a television interview with Gloria Heidi.

District Governors:

1969 – 1970 Wilbur Fox, Florissant, MO

1969 – 1970

8—Wilbur J. Fox
Florissant, Mo.

Wilbur Fox of Florissant, MO becomes District Governor. Illini, Midtown, and Carondelet Clubs celebrate their 25th anniversaries.

Outgoing International President Earl Potter is recognized at the International Convention. Photographs are published of him participating in a Scottish Rite ceremony in Chicago and meeting with the Governor of Hawaii.

July, 1969: After two years, NASA's Apollo program culminates in astronaut Neil Armstrong becoming the first human being to set foot on the moon.

Toastmaster Roy Smith is elected mayor of O'Fallon, IL. Toastmaster Vic Henry is elected Lebanon Township auditor. District Governor Wilbur Fox attends the signing of the Governor of Illinois's Toastmasters Month proclamation in conjunction with the organization's 45th anniversary. Past District Governor Adam Bock represents Region V on the TI Nomination Committee.

Clay-Webster Club is cited for gaining 14 new members. The St. Clair Club once again places in the Top-10 Clubs list, and this year also receives distinction for maintaining the 40-member maximum throughout the Toastmasters year. Harold Proffitt is recognized as the District 8 Outstanding Toastmaster of the Year. Josef Seidel is awarded District 8 Area Governor of the Year.

District 8 is recognized as a Distinguished District for the first time.

The TI Board of Directors announces that the Club Achievement Award program will be replaced by the Club Distinguished Plan, beginning in January, 1971.

The *Toastmaster* magazine provides an insert so members can order a new 30-project, 2-book manual (Communication & Leadership / Advanced Communication & Leadership), which replaces Basic Manual, Advanced Speaker, and Leadership through Speaking. This system establishes the Distinguished Toastmaster designation as the apex of achievement in Toastmasters.

District Governors:

1970 – 1971 Ross Poggenpohl, Lincoln, IL

The Glass Breaker

1970 – 1971

8—Ross L. Poggenpohl
Lincoln, Ill.

Ross Poggenpohl of Lincoln, IL becomes District Governor. The Lincoln-Douglas Club celebrates its 35th anniversary. Athenian celebrates its 30th, Metropolitan its 25th, and Mt. Vernon its 20th. Carlinville and Sunset Clubs celebrate their 15th anniversaries.

Earl Drenner earns his Distinguished Toastmaster Award. District 8 Lt. Governor Josef Seidel is featured in an article of the St. Charles Journal. McDonnell Douglas Club leads the TI Membership Sales charts with 17 new members from July to December.

The District 8, Area 3 speech contest winners – Ed Richfield and Roger Hollrah – are congratulated by U.S. Congressman William Hungate. Toastmaster Fred Williams is re-elected to the Missouri House of Representatives.

Forrest Nelson is District 8 Outstanding Toastmaster of the Year. Tom Dillon is District 8 Area Governor of the Year. St. Clair Club maintains its streak as a Top-10 Club and Presidents-40 Club, finishing its second year at full capacity. Noontoasters is a League Leader on the TI Membership Sales Scoreboard.

Toastmasters International outlines new requirements for educational awards and participation in the International Speech Contest.

A woman named Helen Blanchard is admitted to Toastmasters – as a man, under the alias Homer Blanchard.

Two TI Bylaw and Club Constitution amendments are outlined, both focused on allowing women to join for the first time. Amendment A is to delete MALE and replace MALE with PERSON in the TI Bylaws, which permits women to join any club. Amendment B deletes MALE but permits each club to confine membership to one sex or to have open membership. The TI Board of Directors recommends against approving either proposal.

District Governors:
1971 – 1972 Earl Drenner, DTM, O'Fallon, MO

1971 – 1972

Earl Drenner of O'Fallon, MO becomes District Governor. During his term as D8 Lt. Gov-Education, Earl Drenner was a guest on the KWRE "Coffee Hour" radio program in O'Fallon, MO. Ferguson and Webster Groves Clubs celebrate their 25th anniversaries. Centralia celebrates its 20th. "Toastmaster on the Move" recognized the McDonnell Douglas Club for its outstanding Speechcraft, responsible for a 15 member gain the previous term.

8—Earl W. Drenner, DTM
O'Fallon, Mo.

Past District 8 Governor Adam Bock is elected to the International Board of Directors. He is recognized at the International Convention in Calgary. In the same photo spread, Past District 8 Governor Earl Potter is honored as a Past International President.

Toastmaster James Dean is elected chairman of the St. Louis Chapter of the Society for Technical Communication.

TI again restructures the rules for the International Speech Contest, requiring that participants use only original material and deliver a two-minute impromptu speech to further test their abilities.

Toastmasters International initiates the Ralph C. Smedley Memorial Fund and solicits donations.

Facing a loss of support dues to their discriminatory policies, TI agrees to allow exemptions to their male-only policy in clubs sponsored by or affiliated with the government.

Noontoaster and St. Clair Clubs are recognized as Presidents-40 clubs for maintaining a full 40 members during the year. This is the third consecutive year that St. Clair Club has achieved this status. Gilbert Moorman is D8 Outstanding TM of the Year. Janet Harmon is D8 Area Governor of the Year.

District Governors:

1972 – 1973 PJ Hill, Belleville, IL

1973 – 1974 Josef Seidel, Bridgeton, MO

1972 – 1973

P.J. Hill becomes District Governor. Past District Governor Adam Bock serves as Region V Director. Alton Club celebrates its 30th anniversary.

> The Toastmasters International Board of Directors reverses their stance on discrimination against women, proposing at the International Conference to give clubs the option of open membership. The Board recommends that the proposal be approved.

1973 – 1974

Joseph Seidel becomes District Governor. Commodore Club celebrates its 25th anniversary. Lincoln Trails and Clay-Webster celebrate their 20th. Highland and Greenville celebrate their 10th.

The January, 1974 issue of *Toastmaster* magazine is dedicated to the 50th anniversary of Toastmasters International. It includes letters from U.S. Presidents Richard Nixon and Ronald Reagan.

8. Joseph Seidel
Bridgeton, Mo.

Webster Groves Club's Leadership Night is featured in an article.

> The amendment to allow women to become members by vote of the club is approved, taking the first step toward an organization that practices non-discrimination, half a century after its founding.
>
> By October of 1973, 23% of all Toastmasters clubs have already admitted women.

District Governors:

1974 – 1975 Tom Dillon, DTM, Edwardsville, IL

1975 – 1976 Eugene Tesreau, DTM, Ballwin, MO

1974 – 1975

Tom Dillon of Edwardsville, IL becomes District Governor. Midtown, Carondelet, and Illini Clubs celebrate their 30th anniversaries. Cape Girardeau and Aerospace celebrate their 15th.

Duess are raised from $12 to $18.

Lincoln Trails Club tries an unusual tactic to recruit members: obtaining publicity on a Burger Chef marquee.

8. Tom Dillon, ATM
Edwardsville, Illinois

Mack Stewart is District 8 Outstanding Toastmaster of the Year. Clifford Schall is Area Director of the Year.

April, 1975:

Microsoft is founded by Bill Gates and Paul Allen.

1975 – 1976

Eugene Tesreau of Ballwin, MO becomes District Governor. Lincoln-Douglas Club celebrates its 40th anniversary. Athenian celebrates its 35th, Metropolitan its 30th, McDonnell Douglas and Carlinville their 20th, Taxtoasters and O'Fallon their 15th, and Olney its 10th.

Outgoing District Governor Tom Dillon from O'Fallon Club earns his Distinguished Toastmaster Award.

8. Eugene Tesreau, ATM
Ballwin, Missouri

Winged Word Club provides assistance to a family in need in St. Louis.

District Governors:

1976 – 1977 Virgil Greene, O'Fallon, IL

1976 – 1977

8. Virgil D. Greene
O'Fallon, Illinois

Virgil Greene of O'Fallon, IL becomes District Governor. Webster Grove, Capital, and St. Clair Clubs celebrate their 30th anniversaries. Centralia celebrates their 25th and Winged Word their 15th.

Howard Brandt earns his Distinguished Toastmaster Award.

TI publishes a new inverted organizational chart, showing the member on top and working its way down to the largest sections.

The Board of Directors approves development of a multi-manual system for the Advanced Toastmaster designations, beginning with five specialized manuals focused on different areas of development.

The June, 1977 issue of *Toastmaster* magazine features the article "Women – Good Medicine for a Dying Club," advocating for struggling clubs to open their membership to women.

Wilfred Finuf is District 8 Outstanding Toastmaster of the Year. Robert Clark is Area Governor of the Year.

April, 1977:

The first complete Apple home computer is debuted.

District Governors:

1977 – 1978 Clifford Schahl, Lincoln, IL

1978 – 1979 Ed Richfield, Hillsboro, MO

1977 – 1978

Clifford Schahl of Lincoln, IL becomes District Governor. Alton Club celebrates its 35th anniversary. Ferguson, Downtown, and Tarsus celebrate their 30th. Plus Factor celebrates its 25th, Logan County Agricultural its 20th, and Daniel Boone its 10th.

8. Clifford Schahl, ATM
Lincoln, IL

Outgoing District Governor Eugene Tesreau earns his Distinguished Toastmaster Award. Toastmasters International President Blakely visits District 8. He is photographed with Toastmaster Col. Leon McKinney.

Eugene Tesreau is District 8 Outstanding Toastmaster of the Year. Harry Pleis is Area Director of the Year.

The Board of Directors reports that, as of June, 1977, 81% of clubs are open to women, a 13% increase from the previous term. The magazine publishes an article on "Women at the Top."

1978 – 1979

Ed Richfield of Hillsboro, MO becomes District Governor. Commodore Club celebrates its 30th anniversary, and Lincoln Trails, Clay-Webster, and Jefferson County celebrate their 25th.

Mack Stewart and Wilfred Finuf earn their Distinguished Toastmaster Awards.

8. ED RICHFIELD, ATM
Hillsboro, MO

Diane Reeve is District 8 Outstanding Toastmaster of the Year, making her the first woman to receive this award. Gene Collins is Area Director of the Year.

District 8 is selected as a Distinguished District.

District Governors:
1979 – 1980 Ted Randall, DTM, PID, O'Fallon, IL
1980 – 1981 Phil Vonder Haar, DTM, Webster Groves, MO

1979 – 1980

Ted Randall of O'Fallon, IL becomes District Governor. Midtown and Carondelet Clubs celebrate their 35th anniversaries, Thursday Noon its 25th, and Aerospace and Cape Girardeau their 20th. Collinsville Club is incorporated in Collinsville, IL.

8. TED RANDALL
O'Fallon, IL

M.X. Crouse, Wilbur Fox, and outgoing District Governor Ed Richfield earn their Distinguished Toastmaster Awards.

Clifford Shahl is District 8 Outstanding Toastmaster of the Year. Harold Fieberg is Area Director of the Year.

Ferguson and South County Clubs are recognized as TI President's Top-10 Distinguished Clubs.

District 8 is cited as a Distinguished District.

1980 – 1981

Phil Vonder Haar of Webster Groves, MO becomes District Governor. Metropolitan Club celebrates its 35th anniversary. Monsanto and McDonnell Douglas celebrate their 20th. Columbia Toastmasters Club is incorporated in Columbia, MO.

> December, 1980:
>
> John Lennon, beloved member of worldwide music icons The Beatles, is murdered.

William Newgent, Carl Barth, Jr., Virgil Greene, and George Peo earn their Distinguished Toastmaster Awards.

Howard Brandt is District 8 Toastmaster of the Year. Gary White

> Toastmasters International records a significant impact from women being admitted. The Board of Directors also announces another increase in duess, from $18 to $24.

is Area Director of the Year.

District Governors:

1981 – 1982 Calvin King, East St. Louis, IL; Ted Randall

1981 – 1982

Calvin King, from East St. Louis, IL, becomes the first African-American District Governor. Tragically, he dies while in office and Ted Randall finishes his term. Webster Groves, St. Clair, Capitol Clubs celebrate their 35th anniversaries. Winged Word celebrates its 20th.

8. CALVIN KING, ATM
East St. Louis, IL

Phil Vonder Haar, Gene Collins, and Charles Rogers earn their Distinguished Toastmaster Awards. Katherine Ensor earns her DTM as well, becoming the first known woman in District 8 to do so.

Sidney Towerman is highlighted in *Toastmaster* magazine for his national communication plan, entitled "What's Good With America."

Jean Lebedun represents District 8 at the Region V International Speech Contest. South County Club is recognized as a TI President's Top-10 Distinguished Club.

Phil Vonder Haar is District 8 Outstanding Toastmaster of the Year. The District 8 Eight Ball Bulletin, edited by Vonder Haar, is awarded TI Top-10. Jack Rardin is Area Governor of the Year.

Toastmasters International announces a new 10 project Competent Toastmaster Manual to replace the current 15 project manual. Two additional advanced manuals are made available, and the educational award path is reworked to add new sub designations (Bronze and Silver) and adjust the length of membership requirements for several levels.

September, 1981: Appointed by President Ronald Reagan, Sandra Day O'Connor becomes the first female U.S. Supreme Court Justice.

July, 1983: The FamiCom, or Nintendo Entertainment System, is released in Japan. It would revolutionize the home video game industry.

35

District Governors:

1982 – 1983 Harry Pleis, St. Louis, MO

1983 – 1984 Paul Lloyd, Cape Girardeau, MO

A Time of Great Growth

1982 – 1983

Harry Pleis of St. Louis, MO becomes District Governor. Ferguson, Uptown, and Tarsus celebrate their 35th anniversaries. Lorne Fitts and Stephen Adkins earn their Distinguished Toastmaster Awards. William Newgent, Phil Vonder Haar, and George Peo earn their second DTM's.

8. HARRY PLEIS, ATM
St. Louis, MO

Dr. Jean Lebedun, a professional speaker, is announced to be one of several educational speakers presenting at the Toastmasters International Convention.

George Peo is District 8's Outstanding Toastmaster of the Year. Thomas Moore is Area Director of the Year. District 8 is cited as a Distinguished District.

1983 – 1984

Paul Lloyd of Cape Girardeau, MO becomes District Governor. Commodore Club celebrates its 35th anniversary. Al Ott of O'Fallon Club earns his Distinguished Toastmaster Award.

8. PAUL LLOYD, ATM
Cape Girardeau, MO

TI announces a new 10-project Competent Toastmaster Manual to replace the current 15-project manual. Two additional advanced manuals are made available, and the educational award path is reworked to add Bronze and Silver.

Adam Bock is District 8 Outstanding Toastmaster of the Year. Peggy Isgrigg is Area Director of the Year. District 8 again achieves Distinguished District status.

District Governors:

1984 – 1985 Jack Rardin, Charleston, IL

1984 – 1985

The following members earned their Distinguished Toastmaster Awards:

Bruce Moore (647) – DTM (Aug. 1984)

Terry Maddox (654) – DTM (Oct. 1984)

Nancy Kelly (1957) – DTM (Oct. 1984)

Samuel Randall (994) – DTM (Nov. 1984)

Jack Rardin (1354) – DTM (Nov. 1984)

Ken Stunpf (1267) – DTM (Dec. 1984)

Dick Pennington (2842) – DTM (Feb. 1985)

Willie Summerville (461) – DTM

8. Jack A. Rardin, ATM
Charleston, IL

The October, 1984 issue of *Toastmaster* magazine highlights O'Fallon Club's successful Speechcraft.

The first District conferences are held. Educational sessions at the spring conference include: "The History of D8" by Wilbur Fox, DTM; "Lesson from the World of Marketing" by Mike Mueller; "The Other Side" by Jim Sauer, DTM ID; "Verbal Styles of Great Communicators" by Rich Merson; and "Judging Seminar" by Tom Houston.

Sharon Schwendemann takes first place in District-level International Speech Contest and goes on to represent District 8 at the Regional level, in which she also places first.

> January, 1986: The Space Shuttle *Challenger* explodes during launch, resulting in the loss of all hands and the suspension of the shuttle program for more than two years.

District Governors:

1985 – 1986 Gary White, DTM, Webster Groves, MO

1985 – 1986

Governor: Gary White
Lt. Gov. Ed.:   Charlie Rodgers
Lt. Gov. Admin: Al Ott
MO. South Div A Lt. Gov.: Robert Chunn
Mo. No. Div B Lt. Gov.: Charles Carpenter
Cen. IL Div. C Lt. Gov.: David Smith
IL So. Div. D Lt. Gov.:   Lorraine Newgent
Mo. West Div. E Lt. Gov.: Lois Maddox
Gateway Div. F Lt. Gov.: Willie
Summerville
Communic-8 Editor: Tom Mailey

8. Gary White, ATM
Webster Groves, MO

Distinguished Toastmaster Awards: Lorraine Newgent (994), Gary White (2389), Art Schotman (4587), Dale Fitzpatrick (4587)   Bill Newgent is District 8 Outstanding Toastmaster of the Year. Jerry Troyer is Area Governor of the Year. The Lincoln-Douglas Club celebrates its 50th anniversary.

District 8 is recognized as a Distinguished District.

An interview with District Governor Gary White-

What was the biggest challenge in District 8 during your time as District Governor? The District had experienced several major rifts and Toastmasters were not working together. My challenge was to acknowledge the differences but find common ground so the district could move forward.

What was the largest success in District 8 during your time as District Governor? I feel I laid the foundation of experienced leadership so that my ELG and ALG could continue to be Distinguished. This was the first time that D8 was a Distinguished District three years in a row.

If you had a theme, what was it and what did it mean? "Expand Your Horizons Through Toastmasters" was our motto to get new people involved outside their clubs. Too many times in the past we kept calling on the same people to do things, since they were experienced. We worked to get experienced people to not do themselves, but mentor new people. This worked and we had more new Toastmasters interested in District events.

District Governors:
1986 – 1987 Charles Rogers, DTM, PID, Collinsville, IL

1986 – 1987

Governor:	Charlie Rogers
Lt. Gov. Ed.	Al Ott
Lt. Gov. Admin:	George Peo
MO. South Div A Lt. Gov.:	Morrell Diebold
Mo. No. Div B Lt. Gov.:	Charles Carpenter
Cen. IL Div. C Lt. Gov.:	Clarence Stanley
IL So. Div. D Lt. Gov.:	Alan Lovel
Mo. West Div. E Lt. Gov.:	Jerry Troyer
Gateway Div. F Lt. Gov.:	Willie Summerville
Communic-8 Editor:	Mohamed Alim Kazi

Distinguished Toastmaster Awards:
Lance Richter (994) – DTM (Dec. 1986)
Kelly Weber (5222) – DTM (Jan. 1987)
Paul Lloyd (3804) – DTM (May 1987)
Lois Maddox (493) – DTM (June 1987)
Bill Treece (286) – DTM (July 1987)
Carl Hendrickson (1957) – DTM (July 1987)

The District gets taken out to the ballgame. District 8 has a Day at the Ballpark event on September 26, 1987 to watch the St. Louis Cardinals play their rivals, the Chicago Cubs.

Mohamed Alim Kazi is the D8 Outstanding Toastmaster of the Year. Jerry Troyer is D8 Division Lt. Governor of the Year. George Peterson is Area Governor of the Year.

District Governors:

1987 – 1988 Al Ott, Fairview Heights, IL

1987 – 1988

Governor:	Al Ott
Lt. Gov. Ed.	George Peo
Lt. Gov. Admin:	David Smith
MO. South Div A Lt. Gov.:	Larry Hamilton
Three Rivers Div B Lt. Gov.:	M. Alim Kazi
Prairie Div. C Lt. Gov.:	Clarence Stanley
Great Rivers Div. D Lt. Gov.:	Louis Smith
Mo. West Div. E Lt. Gov.:	Lue Holt
Gateway Div. F Lt. Gov.:	George Peterson
Communic-8 Editor:	Tanya Ferguson

8. Al Ott, DTM
Fairview Heights, IL

Distinguished Toastmaster Awards: David Smith (5196), Lawrence Hamilton (1957), Ruby Rogers (4129), Jane Abbott-Morris (5000), Thomas Kirkpatrick (471), Lora Mae Stewart (1408), Jerry Troyer (4636), Jack Howard (6877).

Plus Factor Club celebrates its 35th anniversary. Daniel Boone celebrates its 20th.

Darlene Lewis is D8 Outstanding TM of the Year. Louis Smith is D8 Lt. Governor of the Year. Ronald Snider is Area Governor of the Year. District 8 is a Distinguished District.

1987Oct Intl Convention Sherry Megan Gary White

Toastmasters International announces changes to the club and district officer structure, creating the VP Membership, VP Public Relations, Lt. Governor Marketing, and Public Relations Officer positions. They also adopt a non-smoking policy for all meetings and sessions at the International Convention.

District Governors:
1988 – 1989 George Peo, DTM, Cape Girardeau, MO

1988 – 1989

Governor:	George Peo
Lt. Gov. Ed.	David Smith
Lt. Gov. Admin:	Lorraine Newgent
MO. South Div A Lt. Gov.:	Stuart Oberheu
Thr. Rivers Div B Lt. Gov.:	Nick Greles
Prairie Div. C Lt. Gov.:	James Gire
Gr. Rivers Div. D Lt. Gov.:	Louis Smith
Mo. West Div. E Lt. Gov.:	Thomas Houston
Gateway Div. F Lt. Gov.:	Ron Snider
Communic-8 Editor:	Keith Woodman

8. George E. Peo, DTM
Cape Girardeau, MO

Lincoln Trails and Jefferson County Clubs celebrate their 35th anniversaries.

Distinguished Toastmaster Awards: Camellia Lewis (Oct. 1988), Jerry Troyer (Oct. 1988 & Nov. 1988), John James Howard (Oct. 1988), Dottie Carlson (Feb. 1989), Marin Blevins (June 1989), Charla Rogers (July 1989), George Peo, Luella Holt

Toastmasters International introduces the Distinguished Club, Area, and Division programs.

John Mohr – D8 Outstanding TM of the Year

Nick Greles, CTM – D8 Div. Lt. Governor of the Year

Ralph Kreigh – D8 Area Governor of the Year

District Governors:
1989 – 1990 David Smith, DTM, Quincy, IL

1989 – 1990

Governor:	David Smith
Lt. Gov. Ed.	Lorraine Newgent
Lt. Gov. Admin:	Nick Greles
MO. South Div A Lt. Gov.:	Robert Darque
Thr. Rivers Div B Lt. Gov.:	Persis Mehta
Prairie Div. C Lt. Gov.:	Martha Drake
Gr. Rivers Div. D Lt. Gov.:	Terry Warner
Mo. West Div. E Lt. Gov.:	Ronald Snider
Gateway Div. F Lt. Gov.:	Ralph Kreigh
Communic-8 Editor:	Bill Mantinband

8. David Smith, DTM
Quincy, IL

Thursday Noon Club celebrates its 35th anniversary. Distinguished Toastmaster Awards: George Peo (3804) – (Aug. 1989), David Smith (5196) – (Sep. 1990)

Richard Chadwick – D8 Outstanding TM of the Year

Persis Mehta – D8 Division Governor of the Year

Charles Carpenter – D8 Area Governor of the Year

Charles McBrian, age 91, captured the Best Speaker Award at the Smedley Hometown Memorial Club 4115-8 in April last year.

The August, 1990 issue of *Toastmaster* magazine includes a biography of Judge Charles McBrian, in honor of his 91st birthday. He has been a member of Toastmasters for 53 years.

November, 1989:

As the Soviet Union dissolves in Europe, the Berlin Wall, which had divided East and West Germany for nearly 30 years, is mostly torn down by citizens of both countries as they are allowed, for the first time, to cross the Iron Curtain. Official reunification of the country occurs within a year.

District Governors:

1990 – 1991 Lorraine Newgent, DTM, Fairview Heights, IL

1990 – 1991

Lorraine Newgent becomes the first Woman District 8 Governor.

Governor: Lorraine Newgent
Lt. Gov. Ed.   Nick Greles
Lt. Gov. Admin: Charles Carpenter
MO. South Div A Lt. Gov.:   Robert Darque
Three Rivers Div B Gov.:   Ted Wear
Prairie Div. C Gov.:   Mercedes Nepute
Great Rivers Div. D Gov.:   Terry Warner
Mo. West Div. E Gov.:   Tom Houston
Gateway Div. F Gov.:   Michael Lewis
Communic-8 Editor: Ralph Kreigh

8. Lorraine Newgent, DTM
Fairview Heights, IL

Carlinville Club celebrates its 35th anniversary, and Noontoasters its 20th. Monsanto Noon Time club (7865) is incorporated in St. Louis, MO. Maritz club (7953) is incorporated in Fenton, MO.

Distinguished Toastmasters: Peris Mehta, Carol Anne Levinson

The new Toastmasters International offices open in Rancho Santa Margarita, California. The Board of Directors approves a motion to change the club year to run from July to June, same as the District year. A new District officer system goes into effect.

Ralph Kreigh – D8 Outstanding TM of the Year
Robert Dargue – D8 Division Governor of the Year
Gregory Andrus – D8 Area Governor of the Year
District 8 - Distinguished District

The Fall Conference, held in Clayton, MO, honors the 50-year history of District 8.

Keith Woodman serves as chair, with Jack Rardin coordinating the 50th anniversary celebration.

Special presentations for the 50-year anniversary include:

"D8 What a Difference It Made"

"Video Interview of CC McBrian"

"Honor Roll of Clubs (1940-1950)"

"Special Recognition to D8's 3 Oldest Clubs"

Clubs present skits on the following topics:

"Young Dr. Smedley – The first 25 Years" by Logan Ag (2808)

"Chronology of the Early Years" by Logan Ag (2808)

"An Indian Summer Story" by Lincoln Trails (1354)

"The Birth of a Newborn (Formation of D30)" by Monsanto (1267)

"1972 – The Year of the Rat (They knew how to throw a conference back then)" by Evening Club (3804)

"What's New (Women – A new side of Toastmasters)" by Plus Factor (1229)

"And the Family Grows (the addition of a new Division to D8)" by Gateway Div.

"In the Beginning (Growth of the Evaluation Program)" by Dick Chadwick

District Governors:

1991 – 1992 Nick Greles, St. Louis, MO

1991 – 1992

Governor:	Nicholas (Nick) Greles
Lt. Gov. Ed. & Training	Charles Carpenter
Lt. Gov. Marketing:	Ted Wear
PRO:	Sally Carpenter
MO. South Div A Gov.:	Wesley Talcott
Three Rivers Div B Gov.:	Greg Andrus
Prairie Div. C Gov.:	Roger Worman
Great Rivers Div. D Gov.:	Larry Miller
Mo. West Div. E Gov.:	Howard Citron
Gateway Div. F Gov.:	Bill Mantinband
Communic-8 Editor:	James Mack

8. Nicholas G. Greles, CTM
St. Louis, MO

August, 1991: The World Wide Web is opened to the public.

Toastmasters International President Jack Gillespie, DTM, and his wife Grace attend the Spring Conference. Gillespie gives the keynote, as well as a presidential address. Electric Toasters club celebrates their 20th anniversary.

Distinguished Toastmasters: Charles Carpenter (7865)

Steve Watkins – D8 Outstanding TM of the Year
Greg Andrus – D8 Division Governor of the Year
Virginia Bolten & Floy Westermeier – D8 Area Gov. of the Year

Tom Houston, ATM, and Ted Randall, DTM, receive Presidential Citations.

District Governor:

1992 – 1993 Charles Carpenter, DTM, St. Louis, MO

1992 – 1993

Governor:	Charles Carpenter
LGET:	Ted Wear
LGM:	Steve Watkins
PRO:	Sally Carpenter
Div A Gov.:	Bruce Korbesmeyer
Div B Gov.:	Lisa Powell
Div. C Gov.:	Roger Worman
Div. D Gov.:	Lynne Williams
Div. E Gov.:	Floy Westermeier
Div. F Gov.:	Carole Breckner
Communic8 Ed.:	James Mack

8 Charles N. Carpenter, DTM
St. Louis, MO

Dick Weber, DTM, receives Presidential Citation from TI President Bough for "tireless work to improve the communication & leadership within D8." Alton Club celebrates its 50th anniversary and Logan Ag Agricultural its 35th. Distinguished Toastmasters: Ernestine Ledbetter (3287), Richard Chadwick (525), Peggy Isgrigg (493), Keith Worman (1957), Nancy Jones (1229), Myra Morris Peo, Ralph Kreigh (4492), Ted Wear (525).

Members from District 8 appear on the cover of the October, 1992 issue of *Toastmaster* magazine. The Board of Directors formally recognizes Leadership Institutes and establishes guidelines.

Judge Charles McBrian is remembered with a biography in the District 8 newsletter. South County is a President's Top-5 Distinguished Club.

John Mohr is a quadruple speech contest winner. He has placed 1st in the International Speech Contest, Humorous Speech Contest, Table Topics Contest, and Evaluation Contest. Mary Hose – D8 Outstanding TM of the Year, Floy Westermeier – D8 Division Governor of the Year and James Schwarz – D8 Area Governor of the Year

District 8 - Distinguished District

District Governors:

1993 – 1994 Ted Wear, DTM, St. Peters, MO

1993 – 1994

Governor:	Ted Wear
LGET:	Steve Watkins
LGM:	Floy Westermeier
PRO:	Wes Talcott
Div A Gov.:	Larry Hamilton
Div B Gov.:	Verlyn Tank
Div. C Gov.:	Nate Randall
Div. D Gov.:	James Schwarz
Div. E Gov.:	Peggy Isgrigg
Div. F Gov.:	Carole Breckner
Communic8 Ed.:	John Mohr

8 Ted Wear, DTM
St. Peters, MO

Glen Knudson leads a special Evaluation Seminar. The pattern speaker for the exercise is Fred Miller of Tarsus club.

Distinguished Toastmasters:

Irita Miller (8511) – DTM

Steve Watkins (4626) – DTM

Verlyn Tank (525) – DTM

The Board of Directors announces that a record number of educational awards were received the previous Toastmaster year.

Michael Lewis – D8 Outstanding TM of the Year

James Schwarz – D8 Division Governor of the Year

Mary Kerwin – D8 Area Governor of the Year

District 8 – Distinguished District

District Governors:
1994 – 1995 Steve Eugene Watkins, DTM, Salem, MO

Into the Digital Age

1994 – 1995

Governor:	Steve Watkins
LGET:	Floy Westermeier
LGM:	Jim Schwarz
PRO:	Chuck Carpenter
Div A Gov.:	Larry Hamilton
Div B Gov.:	Joyce Jackson
Div. C Gov.:	Nathan Randall
Div. D Gov.:	Wes Talcott
Div. E Gov.:	Omer Roberts
Div. F Gov.:	Rosia Primous
Communic8 Ed.:	John Mohr

8 Steve Eugene Watkins, DTM
Salem, MO

Floy Westermeier from District 8 carries the American flag at the opening ceremonies of the Toastmasters International Convention. District 8 holds a Tall Tales Contest at St. Louis's famous Muny theater in Forest Park.

Mid-Town and Carondelet clubs celebrate their 50th anniversaries. Aerospace and High Noon celebrate their 35th. Alpha, West County, and Southwestern Bell celebrate their 20th.

Distinguished Toastmasters: Juan Guzman, Floy Westermeier, Paul Kremer, Carole Breckner, Joseph Hagan, Virginia Veit-Bolten, John Clarence Bettag

The October, 1994 issue of *Toastmaster* magazine presents a short history of the Toastmasters organization.

TI announces an official internet webpage: alt.org.toastmasters.

Talu is a President's Top-5 Distinguished Club.

Paul Kremer – D8 Outstanding TM of the Year

Joyce Jackson – D8 Division Governor of the Year

> TI announces that they have created an official internet webpage: alt.org.toastmasters.

District Governors:

1995 – 1996 Floy Westermeier, DTM, PID, Rolla, MO

1995 – 1996

Governor:	Floy Westermeier
LGET:	Jim Schwarz
LGM:	Jean Inabinett
PRO:	Carole Breckner
Div A Gov.:	Skip Caywood
Div B Gov.:	Ed Rowold
Div. C Gov.:	Lynn Hawk
Div. D Gov.:	Lorraine Newgent
Div. E Gov.:	Myrna Coleman
Div. F Gov.:	Georgia Tolle
Communic8 Ed.:	John Mohr

Floy C. Westermeier, DTM
Rolla, MO

An interview with District 8 Governor Floy Westermeier-

What was the biggest challenge in District 8 during your time as District Governor? Covering the entire District! We had clubs scattered in every far corner of our District, as well as the central part of St. Louis and across the river in Illinois. Two-thirds of the Trio lived in the St. Louis area, while I lived in Rolla, so we did a lot of "meet you half-way" meetings and phone calls. Lot of 2 a.m. arrivals at home on work nights.

What was the largest success in District 8 during your time as District Governor? Leading our team to #9 in the world and then having all the D8 members fill the stage to accept our award when we hosted the International Convention in St. Louis.

If you had a theme, what was it and what did it mean? Building TLC: Teamwork, Leadership, and Communication. We built (TLC) Teamwork, Leadership, and Communication with (TLC) tender loving care.

Mary Kerwin – D8 Outstanding TM of the Year
Edwin Rowold, Jr. – D8 Division Governor of the Year
Anton Vanterpool, II – D8 Area Governor of the Year
Angell Chisholm – D8 Award for Leadership Excellence

District 8 – Select Distinguished District

Volunteers from host District 8 made sure the convention ran smoothly.

Host District Chairman Chuck Carpenter greets delegates.

The Toastmasters International Convention is held in St. Louis, MO; Highlights and photos are featured in the October, 1996 issue of *Toastmaster* magazine. The District holds another "D8 at the Ballpark" day on July 27, 1996.

O'Fallon, Creve Coeur, and McDonnell Douglas clubs celebrate their 35th anniversaries. Salem and Horace Mann celebrate their 20th.

Christine Jarzenbeck of St. Louis publishes the article "Connected: A Toastmaster's Guide to the Internet" in the July, 1996 issue of *Toastmaster* magazine.

D8 awards Able Parliamentarian Certificates to Carole Breckner, Angell Chisholm, Lisa Collier, Walter Collier, George Noll, Jim Schwarz, Steve Watkins, and Ted Wear.

Governor's Education Awards are presented to Cindy Larm and Rosemary Gent.

District Governors:

1996 – 1997 James Schwarz, DTM, Maryland Heights, MO

1996 – 1997

Governor:	James Schwarz
LGET:	Jean Inabinett
LGM:	Ed Rowold
PRO:	Michael Lewis
Div A Gov.:	Diana Jones
Div B Gov.:	Walter Collier
Div. C Gov.:	Lynne Hawk
Div. D Gov.:	Michael Warner
Div. E Gov.:	Cindy Larm
Div. F Gov.:	George Noll
Communic8 Ed.:	John Mohr

James Schwarz, DTM
Maryland Heights, MO

District 54 in central Illinois requests that District 8 cede five counties to them. District 8 declines.

Capitol and St. Clair clubs celebrate their 50th anniversaries. Rent-A-Toast club is incorporated in St. Louis.

Victor Costa achieves Accredited Speaker status. Talu is a President's Top-5 Distinguished club.

DTMs: Francilda Ann Venable Erickson, Jean Inabinett, Myrna Coleman, Marlene Slettehaugh

Lorraine Newgent – D8 Outstanding TM of the Year
Cindy Larm – D8 Division Governor of the Year
Angell Chisholm – D8 Area Governor of the Year

TI provides details on the new and improved education system, which integrates the beginnings of the leadership track into the existing design. June 30, 1999 is the deadline for filing educational awards in the old system. The Board of Directors reworks the criteria for nominating District officers and makes prayer and the pledge optional at meetings.

District Governors:

1997 – 1998 Jean Inabinett, DTM, Maryland Heights, MO

1997 – 1998

Governor: Jean Inabinett
LGET: Ed Rowold
LGM: Carole Breckner
PRO: John Roberts
Div. A Gov.: Diana Jones
Div. B Gov.: Joe McDevitt
Div. C Gov.: Cheryl Hill
Div. D Gov.: Arthur Hampton
Div. E Gov.: Jane Messinger
Div. F Gov.: Angell Chisholm
Communic8 Ed.: Mary Kerwin and Jodi Schierbecker

Jean M. Inabinett, DTM
Maryland Heights, MO

Ferguson and Tarsus clubs celebrate their 50th anniversaries.

The Board of Directors requires that District Officers sign an agreement as a part of the nomination process and prohibits TI candidates from mailing to Districts.

Distinguished Toastmasters:
James Salih (1957) – DTM (Nov. 1997)
Brenda Johnmeyer (4043) – DTM (Nov. 1997)
Jane Messenger (1056) – DTM (Jan. 1998)

Floy Westermeier – D8 Outstanding TM of the Year
Angell Chisholm – D8 Division Governor of the Year
Dori Drummond – D8 Area Governor of the Year
District 8 – Distinguished District

The Board of Directors requires that District Officers sign an agreement as a part of the nomination process and prohibits TI candidates from mailing to Districts.

District Governors:

1998 – 1999 Edwin Rowold, Jr., DTM, Chesterfield, MO

1998 – 1999

Governor:	Edwin Rowold, Jr.
LGET:	Carole Breckner
LGM:	Nate Randall
PRO:	Anita Harding
Div. A Gov.:	Tom Coscia
Div. B Gov.:	Wayne Mosher
Div. C Gov.:	Jean Inabinett
Div. D Gov.:	Reva Mueggenberg
Div. E Gov.:	Joyce Kelly
Div. F Gov.:	Shash Bhave
Communic8 Ed.:	Mary Kerwin

Edwin Rowold Jr., ATM-B
Chesterfield, MO

District 8 creates its own website: D8Toastmasters.org.

Decatur Commodore club celebrates its 50th anniversary. Metro East and Good Neighbor celebrate their 20th.

University of Missouri Rolla is a President's Top-5 Distinguished club.

Earl Potter, Past District 8 Governor and International President, passes away in Bowling Green, Kentucky. He is survived by his wife, Helen.

Several new sets of standards for club, area, division, and district officers are presented. The Board of Directors limits campaign speeches to the district spring conference.

DTMs: Ana Anita Atok, Shashikant Bhave, John Easterling Roberts, Jr.

Charles Rogers – Outstanding TM of the Year

Shasikant Bhave – Division Governor of the Year

Cheryl Norsic – Area Governor of the Year

District 8 – Distinguished District

District Governors:

1999 – 2000 Carole Breckner, DTM, Arnold, MO

1999 – 2000

Governor:	Carole Breckner
LGET:	Cindy Larm
LGM:	Shash Bhave
PRO:	Kathy Cissell
Division A Gov.:	Jim Noonan
Division B Gov.:	Raghavan Rajagopalan
Division C Gov.:	Jeffry Maxwell
Division D Gov.:	Michael Stewart
Division E Gov.:	Fran Erickson
Division F Gov.:	Kelly Stohl
Communic8 Ed.:	Gary White

Carole Breckner, DTM
Arnold, MO

The *Toastmasters* magazine features several special presentations in honor of the 75th anniversary of Toastmasters International. Among them are a biography of founder Ralph Smedley, the development of the first Basic Manual, and a history of the Toastmistress organization and their transition into Toastmasters.

Collinsville, Fairview Heights, and Smedley Hometown clubs celebrate their 20th anniversaries.

Lora Mae Stewart receives a Presidential Citation at the TI Convention for establishing the first "Inmate Toastmasters Club."

Distinguished Toastmasters: Michael Warner (4129), Floy Westermeier (1056), Ed Rowold, Jr. (6629), Nathaniel Randall (51), Rosia Primous (4345), Tom Coscia (4938).

Angell Chisholm – Outstanding TM of the Year

Kelly Stohl – Division Governor of the Year

Richard "Dick" Chadwick – Area Governor of the Year

District 8 – Distinguished District

An interview with District 8 Governor Carole Breckner, DTM-

What was the biggest challenge in District 8 during your time as District Governor? Trying to keep the momentum going from the previous District Governors. Floy Westermeir - Select Distinguished; Jean Inabinett - Distinguished; Ed Rowald Distinguished? I wanted to keep the tradition going.

Carole Breckner & TI President

What was the largest success in District 8 during your time as District Governor? District 8 was Distinguished District in 1999-2000; we missed Select Distinguished by one point. Everyone pulled together to achieve ALL the goals.

If you had a theme, what was it and what did it mean? My theme was "Commitment Is the Key to Success." In my career as a Toastmaster, I was committed to find out ALL aspects of the organization, and that included the history of past administrations in District 8. Understanding the past will enhance the future of the District.

Secondly, what worked for previous administrations were used and the not so good decisions were discarded. Third, keeping the entire District informed of the goals of Toastmasters International and passing them to the Division, Area, and the Clubs. Requesting all participants achieve their personal goals would advance the Area and Division Goals.

Aug 2000 TI Convention, Miami Beach, FL.
Lora Mae Stewart Receives Presidential Citation for Establishing the First Inmate Toastmasters Club

Most Importantly, I thoroughly enjoyed working with my teams. When we achieved Distinguished District, I congratulated all the members. I was almost to tears when I did that at the Council Meeting in 2000.

Members of the Top Five Club winning University of Missouri Club 4850-8 from Rolla, Missouri, accept their award from President Daily during the Hall of Fame ceremony.

Aug 2000 TI Convention, Miami Beach, FL
D8 Receives Distinguished District, Excellence in Education & Training and Excellence in Marketing Plaques
Carole Breckner, Cindy Larm, Floy Westermeier, Shash Bhave

District Governors:
2000 – 2001 Cindy Larm, DTM, Booneville, MO

Mastering the New Millennium

2000 - 2001

Governor:	Cindy Larm
LGET:	Shash Bhave
LGM:	Omer Roberts*
PRO:	Mary Kerwin
Division A Gov.:	David Shanahan*
Division B Gov.:	Dick Chadwick
Division C Gov.:	Roger Worman
Division D Gov.:	Michael Stewart
Division E Gov.:	Dori Drummond
Division F Gov.:	Angell Chisholm*
Communic8 Ed.:	Gary White

Cindy Larm, DTM
Booneville, MO

* = Appointed when the original holder of office resigned.

An interview with District Governor Cindy Larm, DTM-

What was the biggest challenge in District 8 during your time as District Governor? My biggest challenge was continuing to maintain positive energy and minimum disruptions for everyone while keeping leadership in place. We had a few challenges with leadership changes and absences throughout my term.

What was the largest success in District 8 during your time as District Governor? My biggest success was the camaraderie and friendships that we formed. Through this, we were able to keep positive momentum going with everyone working together, despite the obstacles thrown out.

If you had a theme, what was it and what did it mean? My theme was "Friends Making the Difference." My hope was for members to see us as friends and family, helping each other to learn and grow through Toastmasters, while having some fun at the same time.

Lord Effingham, Columbia, and Anheuser Busch clubs celebrate their 20th anniversaries. Division D is dissolved dues to decline in number and strength of clubs. The remaining clubs are absorbed into Division A.

Distinguished Toastmasters:

Asasu Chellaiah (2516) – DTM (Sept. 2000)

Carole Breckner (3268) – DTM (Dec. 2000)

Jim Noonan (1957) – DTM (June 2001)

Dave Shanahan (7865) – DTM (July 2001)

John Mohr (2389) – DTM (July 2001)

Joyce Jackson – D8 Outstanding TM of the Year

Dori Drummond – D8 Division Governor of the Year

David Mallory – D8 Area Governor of the Year

May 2000 D8 Spring Conference
Incoming D8 Officers
Floy Westermeier, DTM(ID), Carole Breckner, DTM(IPDG), Cindy Larm, DTM(DG),
Shash Bhave, DTM (LGET), Kelly Stohl, DTM(LGM)[Resigned Jun2000]

September 11, 2001:

Terrorists hijack commercial aircraft and crash them into the World Trade Center towers in New York City and the Pentagon in Washington, D.C., resulting in approximately 9000 casualties. The attacks define the following decades, and their effects are still being felt to this day.

District Governors:
2001 – 2002 Shashikant Bhave, DTM, Fenton, MO

2001 – 2002

Governor: Shashikant Bhave
LGET: Omer Roberts
LGM: George Noll
PRO: Mary Kerwin
Division AD Gov.:   David Shanahan
Division B Gov.:   Nancy Jones
Division C Gov.:   Pamela Wickman
Division E Gov.:   Fran Erickson
Division F Gov.:   Cheryl Norsic
Communic8 Ed.:   Carole Breckner

Shashikant Bhavé, DTM
Fenton, MO

Waynesville-St. Robert, Ozark Orators, University of Missouri-Rolla, and Capital T Toastmasters clubs celebrate their 20th anniversaries. Fort Leonard Wood celebrates its 35th.

Distinguished Toastmasters:
Walter "Renegade" Collier, Jr. (525) – DTM (Dec. 2001)
Thomas Marcy (4492) – DTM (Apr. 2002)
Michael Lewis (4928) – DTM (Apr. 2002)
Joyce Kelly (4043) – DTM
Carole Breckner – D8 Outstanding TM of the Year
Cheryl Passanise – D8 Division Governor of the Year
Michael Lewis – D8 Area Governor of the Year
Joe Passanise – Retired Toastmaster of the Year

District Governors:

2002 – 2003 Omer Roberts, DTM, Jefferson City, MO

2002 – 2003

Governor:	Omer Roberts
LGET:	George Noll
LGM:	Nancy Jones
PRO:	Carol Warner
Division AD Gov.:	Dan Darnall
Division B Gov.:	Mary Kerwin
Division C Gov.:	Pamela Wickman
Division E Gov.:	David Mallory
Division F Gov.:	Michael Lewis
Communic8 Ed.:	Carole Breckner

Omer Roberts, DTM
Jefferson City, MO

"My theme for this year fits with our International President Gavin Blakey's theme of "Toastmasters Bringing Out The Best In People." I freely borrowed from President Blakey and from the symbol of our part of the country, the Gateway Arch, for my theme. I truly believe that this organization is the 'Gateway to Your Best' and that we will see our members strive for their best in the remaining months of our year. I am confident that you will continue our District's tradition of achieving educational objectives for CTMs, ATMs, DTMs, and leadership awards. And I also believe that most of those who achieve their first CTM will see the value in continuing in the Advanced C&L programs." - Dist. Gov. Omer Roberts

Plus Factor club celebrates its 50th anniversary. Grand Center celebrates its 20th.

Dr. Steve Watson, DTM receives a Presidential Citation.

DTMs: Joyce Kelly, Carol Warner.

Terry Rolan – D8 Outstanding TM of the Year (TM Oct 2003)

Michael Lewis – D8 Division Governor of the Year (TM Oct 2003)

Janet Harmon – D8 Area Governor of the Year (TM Oct 2003)

Ken Oster – D8 Retired Toastmaster of the Year

District Governors:
2003 – 2004 George Noll, St. Louis, MO

2003 – 2004

Governor:	George Noll
LGET:	Nancy Jones
LGM:	Mary Kerwin
PRO:	Mary Kerwin
Division AD Gov.:	Alison Baker
Division B Gov.:	Bob Gergen
Division C Gov.:	Carole Breckner
Division E Gov.:	Vicki Miserez
Division F Gov.:	Joe Passanise

8 George Noll, ATM-G
St. Louis, MO

Ken Degler Lincoln Trails club celebrates its 50th anniversary. **TI announces that duess can now be paid online.**

Distinguished Toastmasters:

Dori Drummond (4590) – DTM (Sept. 2003)

Robert Gergen (3227) – DTM (Nov. 2003)

Mary Kerwin (3227) – DTM (Nov. 2003)

Oliver Richards (7953) – DTM (Mar. 2004)

Daniel Darnall (4590) – DTM (July 2004)

Frank Martelli (7865) – DTM (July 2004)

Carol Warner – D8 Outstanding TM of the Year

Robert Gergen – D8 Division Governor of the Year

Terry Ryan – D8 Area Governor of the Year

TI announces that duess can now be paid online.

A
> February, 2004:
>
> The social networking website Facebook goes online.

message from District Governor George Noll-

During my term as District Governor, I have been impressed with the dedication and resourcefulness of the people in Toastmasters. The District 8 team accomplished a lot during the year, with record club officer training numbers at TLl, two great District conferences, and

61

successes in the education program with large numbers of new CTMs, ATMs, and DTMs. Thirteen clubs were Distinguished, ten were Select Distinguished, and an astounding nineteen were Presidential Distinguished. In addition, five areas reached the Distinguished Area, four reached Select Distinguished, and three were Presidential Distinguished. Division B achieved the honor of Presidential Distinguished Division and E received Select Distinguished. Congratulations for the hard work and dedication of the outstanding Toastmasters responsible for these achievements.

While District failed to achieve the Distinguished classification last year, we greatly surpassed our educational goals with 136 new CTMs and an outstanding number of 92 ATM awards. There were also 54 Competent Leaders, nine Advanced Leaders, seven Distinguished Toastmasters and eight Leadership Excellence awards presented to members of District 8. Our Lt. Governor of Education, Nancy Jones, DTM, received the Excellence in Education award from TI for her efforts.

We also were pleased to welcome five new clubs to our ranks. These were Southern Illinois, St. Louis Association of Realtors, ScriptMasters, Square Talkers, and AMD. Even with the five new clubs, we failed to reach our membership goals because of clubs that we lost throughout the year. Once again, I would like to express my thanks and admiration to those people that worked hard to provide the District with a great Toastmasters Experience.

We could not do without the many committee chairs and committee members behind the scenes who made things work, as well as the dedicated Area and Division Governors that kept things moving. I am passing the gavel on to your new District Governor, Nancy Jones, confident that she will bring District 8 to new heights.

The Board of Directors establishes that areas should consist of four to six clubs. They also announce duess increase from $24 to $27.

District Governors:
2004 – 2005 Nancy Jones, DTM, St. Louis, MO

2004 – 2005

Governor:	Nancy Jones
LGET:	Mary Kerwin
LGM:	Michael Lewis
PRO:	Rosia Primous
Division AD Gov.:	Sandy Swearingen
Division B Gov.:	Tony Gartner
Division C Gov.:	Qaiser Khan
Division E Gov.:	Carol Buening
Division F Gov.:	Jim Tayon
Communic8 Ed.:	Omer Roberts

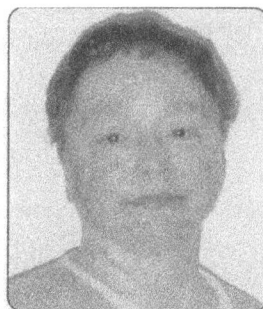

Nancy Lee Jones, DTM
Saint Louis, MO

An interview with District Governor Nancy Jones, DTM-

If you had a theme, what was it and what did it mean? We can feel the energy in District 8. Examples of success are shining through. It is seen in the Membership, Education, and Administration. We need to focus on each member getting the most of their Toastmasters benefits. If each member, each club, each area, and each division does this, everyone will reap rewards. Everyone (including District 8) will be Distinguished. Join me and your new district leadership team as we "Ignite the Light!"

Thursday Noon club celebrates its 50th anniversary. The Board of Directors establishes that areas should consist of four to six clubs. They also announce a dues increase, from $24 to $27. Wes Talcott receives the Governor's Special Service Award.

DTMs: Bob Glidewell, Anna Pennington, Denise Gerst, Vicky Miserez, Ronald Kautzner, Alison Baker, Qaisar Khan

Bob Gergen – D8 Outstanding TM of the Year

Tony Gartner – D8 Division Governor of the Year

Sharon Scott-Moyer – D8 Area Governor of the Year

Lorraine Newgent - Retired Toastmaster of the Year

District Governors:

2005 – 2006 Mary Kerwin, DTM, Wildwood, MO

2005 – 2006

Governor:	Mary Kerwin	
LGET:	Dan Darnall	
LGM:	Barbara Kryvko	
PRO:	Ollie Richards	
Division A Gov.:	Dale Lancaster	
Division B Gov.:	Sharon Scott-Moyer	
Division C Gov.:	Pamela Wickman	
Division E Gov.:	Ralph Kreigh	
Division F Gov.:	Kevin Desrosiers	
Communic8 Ed.:	Omer Roberts (Until his death)	

McBrian Lincoln-Douglas club (renamed in honor of longtime member Judge Charles McBrian) celebrates its 70th anniversary. Mallinckrodt celebrates its 35th.

DTMs: Tom Coscia, Cheryl Passanise, Joseph Passanise, Barbara Kryvko, Marlyn Whitney, Diana Ross, Tammy Fadler, Ruth Halbach, Terry Rolan, Kevin Desrosiers.

May 2006 D8 Spring Conference
Kevin Desrosiers, DTM   Bernadine Chapman
Divison Gov. of the Year   Area Governor of the Year

Dawn Tucker – D8 Outstanding TM of the Year

Kevin Desrosiers – D8 Division Governor of the Year

Bernadine Chapman – D8 Area Governor of the Year

Nancy Jones – Retired Toastmaster of the Year

TI rolls out the new educational program, divided into communication and leadership manuals at the basic and advanced levels. The Board of Directors changes the purpose of District Conferences, and they introduce FreeToastHost, a program to allow clubs to create their own websites.

August, 2005: Hurricane Katrina hits the Southeastern United States, causing nearly 2000 deaths and unprecedented financial devastation.

District Governors:

2006 – 2007 Dan Darnall, DTM, Fenton, MO

2006 – 2007

Governor:	Dan Darnall
LGET:	Barbara Kryvko
LGM:	Tony Garner
PRO:	Ollie Richards
Division A Gov.:	Jerry Hoeflein
Division B Gov.:	Susan Harrington
Division C Gov.:	Eileen Kluckman
Division E Gov.:	Cindy Larm
Division F Gov.:	Denise Gerst
Communic8 Ed.:	Rosemary Jermann and Adrienne Schlegel

An interview with District Governor Dan Darnall, DTM-

What was the biggest challenge in District 8 during your time as District Governor? The biggest challenge we had was to get people to participate outside the club.

What was the largest success in District 8 during your time as District Governor? Though we ended up 60 people short of being distinguished, the district as a whole put plans in place to reach success in coming years.

If you had a theme, what was it and what did it mean? My theme was "Let it Shine." The purpose was to find your passion; kindle the fire and let it shine.

FRB club celebrates its 20th anniversary.

The Board of Directors makes a proposal to move duess from Bylaws to Policy, enabling them to raise duess without a vote of the membership. They also declare that ratification by email is acceptable if a quorum is not reached at the district conference.

Distinguished Toastmasters:

Orrin Dieckmeyer (4345) – DTM (Sep. 2006)

Carolyn Buening (4492) – DTM (Feb. 2007)

Gerald Buening (4492) – DTM (Feb. 2007)

Bernadine Chapman (Voices in Unity)

Ruth Halback (Rent-a-Toast)

Wayne Mosher (Midtown Clayton)

Allan Gerber (2905) – DTM (July 2007)
Ethel Scoggin (5000) – DTM (July 2007)
Daniel Darnall (7953) – DTM (July 2007)
Eileen Kluckman (Noontime)

Kevin Desrosiers – D8 Outstanding TM of the Year
Sue Harrington – D8 Division Governor of the Year
Dawn Tucker and Cindy Hoeflein – D8 Area Governor of the Year
Mary Kerwin – Retired Toastmaster of the Year

District Governors:
2007 – 2008 Barbara Kryvko, DTM, St. Charles, MO

2007 – 2008

Governor:	Barbara Kryvko
LGET:	Tony Garner
LGM:	Dori Drummond
PRO:	Daryl Sutphen
Division A Gov.:	Thomas Donavan
Division B Gov.:	Dawn Tucker
Division C Gov.:	Dale Fitzpatrick
Division E Gov.:	Mary Young
Division F Gov.:	Lora Mather
Communic8 Ed.:	Rosemary Jermann (Issues 1&2) and Adrienne Schlegel (Issue 1)

Life Sciences and Tax Toasters clubs celebrate their 20th anniversaries.

Distinguished Toastmasters:
Wayne Allen (4431) – DTM (Sep. 2007)
Dawn Tucker (9677) – DTM (Sep. 2007)
Herman Koester (496) – DTM (Dec. 2007)
Angela Young (4345) – DTM (Dec. 2007)
Gerald Hoeflein (930005) – DTM (Dec. 2007)
Kenton De Motte (701931) – DTM (Feb. 2008)
Roberta Anderson (9793) – DTM (Mar. 2008)
Steven Hand (9793) – DTM (Mar. 2008)
Tony Gartner (9677) – DTM (May 2008)
Debbie Hyde (5585) – DTM (June 2008)
Margaret Walker – D8 Outstanding TM of the Year
Dawn Tucker – D8 Division Governor of the Year
Sly Brooks – D8 Area Governor of the Year
District 8 – Distinguished District

District Governors:
2008 – 2009 Tony Gartner, DTM, St. Peters, MO

2008 – 2009
Governor: Tony Gartner
LGET: Dori Drummond
LGM: Tim Spezia

The *Toastmaster* magazine stops listing Club Anniversaries and DTM awards.

TI announces that the 2010 International Convention planned for Sydney, Australia, has been moved to Palm Desert dues to the 2008 Financial Crisis.

Dan Darnall – D8 Outstanding TM of the Year

Curtis Scroggins – D8 Division Governor of the Year

Kathryn Mokriakow – D8 Area Governor of the Year

District8 – Distinguished District

Tony Gartner with District 8 Toastmasters – May 2015 Spring Conference.

District Governors:
2009 – 2010 Dori Drummond, DTM, Jefferson City, MO

2009 – 2010
Governor:	Dori Drummond
LGET:	Tim Spezia
LGM:	John Barry
Division A Gov.:	Carole Breckner
Division B Gov.:	Kathryn Mokriakow
Division C Gov.:	Randy Lanning
Division F Gov.:	Eileen Roth
Communic8 Ed.:	Joann York and Daryl

Sutphen

Toastmasters presents a historical overview for its 85th anniversary. A Toastmasters podcast is discussed in the April, 2010 issue of *Toastmaster*.

Members throughout St. Louis take part in the St. Patrick's Day

Parade.

Distinguished Toastmasters: Todd Austin, Robert Bob Gergen, Cindy Hoeflein, Daryl Sutphen, Jennifer Merritt, Stanley Veyhl

Joann York – D8 Outstanding TM of the Year

Curtis Scroggins & Kathryn Mokriakow – D8 Div. Gov. of the Year

D.J. Randle & Raymond Allen – D8 Area Governor of the Year

Robert Blattman – Retired Toastmaster of the Year

Curtis Scroggins & Kathryn Mokriakow – D8 Division Governor of the Year. D.J. Randle and Raymond Allen – D8 Area Governor of the Year

District 8 – Select Distinguished District

District Governors:
2010 – 2011 Tim Spezia, DTM, St. Louis, MO

2010 – 2011

Governor:	Tim Spezia
LGET:	Tom Coscia
LGM:	Curtis Scroggins
PRO:	Jeanette Lynch
Division A Gov.:	Lora Mather
Division B Gov.:	Jacquie Vick
Division C Gov.:	Larry Hemingway, Sr.
Division E Gov.:	Cynthia Scroggins
Division F Gov.:	Raymond Allen
Communic8 Ed.:	Joann York

The Traveling Toastmaster segment of *Toastmaster* magazine features a picture of Lt. Gov. Tom Coscia in the February, 2011 issue. Toastmasters throughout St. Louis march in the St. Patrick's Day

Parade.

Distinguished Toastmasters: Lydia Pochedly, Terry Calderwood, Dossie Randle. Jeanette M. Lynch – D8 Outstanding TM of the Year , Lora Mather – D8 Division Governor of the Year . Debra Morrissey – D8 Area Governor of the Year. John Barry – D8 Retired Toastmaster of the Year   **District 8 – Distinguished District**

District Governors:
2011 - 2012 Tom Coscia, DTM, St. Peters, MO

2011 – 2012

Governor:	Tom Coscia
LGET:	Curtis Scroggins
LGM:	Lora Mather
PRO:	Kat Mokriakow
Division A Gov.:	Debra Morrissey
Division B Gov.:	Dossie (D.J.) Randle
Division C Gov.:	Larry Hemingway, Sr.
Division E Gov.:	Pam Melloway
Division F Gov.:	Sandra Kardis
Communic8 Ed.:	Joann York and Cynthia Scroggins

An interview with District Governor Tom Coscia, DTM-

What was the biggest challenge in District 8 during your time as District Governor? Annual membership duess were increased while I was District Governor.

What was the largest success in District 8 during your time as District Governor? We allowed new DTM recipients to have a mentor/friend speak about them and allowed the recipient to give a short thank you speech. This has made a more meaningful ceremony, which will hopefully inspire more people to earn their DTM. For the first time, the District awarded two corporate recognitions (Maritz and Enterprise) to build PR and a stronger relationship with our corporate partners. *(See next page.)*

If you had a theme, what was it and what did it mean? I was the first year the DG was not allowed to have a theme!

The 1999 World Champion of Public Speaking, Craig Valentine, in town for an engagement with the National Speakers Association, holds a workshop on storytelling for District 8.

Distinguished Toastmasters: Paul Cook, Sandy Kardis, Benedict Kemper, Ralph Morrissey, Debra Morrissey, Jackie Vick, Nathan Randall, Becka Clark, Richard Hawkins, Karen Cupp, Lora Mather, Curtis Scroggins, Cynthia Scroggins, Jane Clark.

On May 18th, International Director Andy Little presented corporate recognition, a beautiful crystal globe, to Steve Maritz, chairman and CEO of Maritz, and Nina McVey, Associate VP with Enterprise Holdings.

Corporate recognitions reinforce the relationship between Toastmasters and these corporate sponsors by providing physical recognition of Toastmasters International's appreciation of the sponsoring organization's support. Only an International Officer or Director may present corporate awards. Toastmasters International requires that corporations receiving this award must: support more than one Toastmasters club or have the potential to sponsor more clubs and have a high profile in the community, such as a major employer or a local government agency.

Since Nov. 1990, Maritz has supported Toastmasters by chartering the Maritz Toastmasters Club # 7953. In Jan. 2002, a second club was chartered — Speak Easy Toastmasters Club # 5585.

Enterprise Holdings was recognized for their support for three Toastmaster clubs — Rent-A-Toast Club # 8399, WelDon Toastmasters Club # 851506, and the recently chartered Toast On the Rock Club # 2264661.

Kat Mokriakow – D8 Outstanding TM of the Year
Debra Morrissey – D8 Division Governor of the Year
Peggy Willoughby – D8 Area Governor of the Year
Sandra Kardis – D8 Retired Toastmaster of the Year

District Governors:

2012 – 2013 Curtis Scroggins, DTM, Jefferson City, MO

2012 – 2013

Governor:	Curtis Scroggins
LGET:	Lora Mather
LGM:	Sandra Kardis
Division A Gov.:	Mike Kotur
Division B Gov.:	Cynthia Warren
Division C Gov.:	Jef Williams
Division E Gov.:	Frank Yates
Division F Gov.:	Jeannette Lynch
Communic8 Ed.:	Joann York

What was the biggest challenge in District 8 during your time as District Governor? My biggest challenge in District 8 during my time as District Governor was achieving the number of membership payments required to become Distinguished.

What was the largest success in District 8 during your time as District Governor? My greatest success in District 8 during my time as District Governor was the spike in attendance during the District Conferences. We had some of the most well-attended conferences up to that point during my year as District Governor.

If you had a theme, what was it and what did it mean? We were not allowed to have a theme, but my unofficial theme was inclusion, and we had a pin that demonstrated it, using the number 8 in the middle of the pin with the curve of the 8 signifying the Mississippi river running between Illinois and the upper/lower parts of the number indicating the Illinois/Missouri parts of the District, respectively.

DTM's: Dan Darnall, Peggy Willoughby, Cynthia Warren, William Levins, Talfanita Cobb, Darlene Suter, Debra Morrissey, Chandan Unchageri, Casetta Stevens, Robin Anderson, Jeanette Lynch, George Noll, Brenda English, Barbara Kryvko.

Mike Kotur – D8 Outstanding TM of the Year
Jeanette Lynch – D8 Division Governor of the Year
Taffy Cobb – D8 Area Governor of the Year
Carole Breckner – Retired Toastmaster of the Year

District Governors:

2013 – 2014 Lora Mather, DTM, Chesterfield, MO

2013 – 2014

Governor:	Lora Mather
LGET:	Sandra Kardis
LGM:	Debra Morrissey
PRO:	Farzana Chohan
Division A Gov.:	Stuart Welter
Division B Gov.:	Kenneth Freeman
Division C Gov.:	Howard Price
Division E Gov.:	Richard Porter
Division F Gov.:	Ralph Morrissey
Communic8 Ed.:	Joann York with

photographer Chuck Carpenter

In the September, 2013 issue of *Toastmaster* magazine's Meet My Mentor section, Mike Kotur relates how he benefitted from his mentor, former District Governor Dan Darnall.

Distinguished Toastmasters:

Michael Kotur	Howard Lee Price
Jeffrey Williams	Yolandea Wood
William Kurt Minton	Lawson Calhoun
Leanne Waugh	Gert Baldwing
Kenneth Dan Freeman	Sandra Kardis
Bill Burlison	Wendy Clothier
Joann York	David Mallory
Thomas Ahillen	Philip Mette
Farzana Chohan	Jason Obert
Stuart Welter	Bridgette Wesley
Larry Hemingway	

Jerry Chapman – D8 Outstanding TM of the Year
Howard Price – D8 Division Governor of the Year
Tom Gillard – D8 Area Governor of the Year
Ralph Morrissey – Retired Toastmaster of the Year

An interview with District Governor Lora Mather, DTM-

What was the biggest challenge in District 8 during your time as District Governor? My biggest challenge was that the May Business Meeting was scheduled to be held in Jefferson City. In the past, it had been difficult to get a quorum present for the vital business of electing district leaders and the club realignment action. Thanks to getting the word out early and to our club presidents and VPE's, we had a quorum plus 10 present to conduct business. This was a big challenge that was met successfully and District 8 amended procedures to avoid having the May Business meeting outside the metro area.

Prior to my election as District Governor District 8 suffered a loss of Dori Drummond and this was a very hard blow. I hope that somewhere in the District 8 history will be a special place for our leaders who have left this earth.

What was the largest success in District 8 during your time as District Governor? The success during my time was the achievement of 14 DTMs. Most other districts only have 4-6 DTMs awarded and celebrated. The number of DTM's speaks well of the members of District 8 and their ability to mentor and help each other to achieve the highest educational awards in the organization.

If you had a theme, what was it and what did it mean? No theme. But I like airplanes and flying and use a by-line as "Together We Fly Higher."

Lora Mather with the past District Governor, Curtis Scroggins.

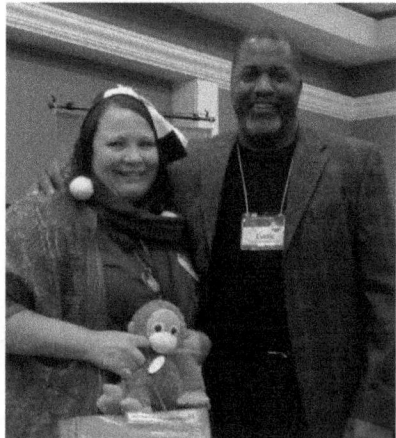

District Governors:
2014 – 2015 Sandy Kardis, DTM, St. Louis, MO

2014 – 2015

Governor:	Sandra Kardis
LGET:	Farzana Chohan
LGM:	Jacquie Vick
PRO:	Gina Willard
Division A Gov.:	Adam Kutell
Division B Gov.:	Carol Steinbach
Division C Gov.:	Tom Gillard
Division E Gov.:	Kenneth Freeman
Division F Gov.:	Regina Dennis
Communic8 Ed.:	Joann York

Distinguished Toastmasters: Neva Nichols, Alan Ayers, Dan Filla, Ralph Kreig, Nancy Suelflow, Jerry Chapman, Carrie Radnov, Kathryn Mokriakow

The *Toastmaster* magazine celebrates the organization's 90th anniversary. A time capsule includes a photograph of Past District 8 Director and International President Earl Potter with California Governor Ronald Reagan. Included in a collection of pins from past TI Conventions is a St. Louis pin.

An interview with District Governor Sandra Kardis-

What was the biggest challenge in District 8 during your time as District Governor? My biggest challenge in District 8 during my time as District Governor was how to mentor/advise the LGET and LGM. Both individuals served in the role of district PRO; however, both were new as members of the District Trio. I could have micro-managed their responsibilities but chose to rely on several things. I shared my experiences as LGM and LGET. I relied on knowledge they would gain from TI Leadership Training. I reinforced knowledge of TI policies and procedures. Finally, I expected personal creativity and commitment they would bring to their roles.

What was the largest success in District 8 during your time as District Governor? My largest success in District 8 during my time as District Governor was updating District 8 membership on the history, current status, and future of the Omer Roberts/Dori Drummond Inmate Scholarship Fund and convincing them to continue fundraising for the continuance of the fund for inmates' duess assistance. I believe I convinced them. As the 2015 - 2016 Omer Roberts/Dori Drummond Inmate Scholarship Fund Ambassador, I was able to collect $772.43 at club meetings, the DEC meeting, and numerous area/division speech contests. District 8 Toastmasters proved they are not only outstanding communicators and leaders but are truly generous individuals.

Frank Yates – D8 Outstanding TM of the Year

Tom Gillard – D8 Division Governor of the Year

Lisa Cooksey-Cannon & Lorie Kaplan – D8 Area Gov. of the Year

Chuck Carpenter & John Mohr – Retired Toastmaster of the Year

Toastmasters International decided to modernize the district leader titles based on the findings of a Board of Directors committee studying the competencies required for district leaders to successfully fulfill their roles to better reflect their responsibilities and real-world practice. Toastmasters International is now in alignment with the organization's strategic plan objective to modernize the programs with a renewed focus on leadership.

District Director:

2015 – 2016 Farzana Chohan, DTM, St. Louis, MO

2015 – 2016

District Director:　　　　Farzana Chohan
Program Quality Director: Jacquie Vick
Club Growth Director:　 Kat Mokriakow
PRO:　　　　　　　　 Camesha Hill-Carter
Division A Dir.:　　　　　Larry Kimborw
Division B Dir.:　　　　　Bridgette Wesley
Division C Dir.:　　　　　James Childress
Division E Dir.:　　Jean Craft
Division F Dir.:　　Pierre Smith
Communic8 Ed.:　　Joann York

First Directors under Toastmasters International new leadership titles

District 8 – Select Distinguished District

Parasarum Ananthram – D8 Outstanding TM of the Year
Bridgette Wesley – D8 Division Director of the Year
Don Smith – Area Director of the Year

Distinguished Toastmasters: Dan Darnall, Ron Gossen, Carol Steinbeck, Frank Yates.

An interview with District Governor Director Farzana Chohan, DTM-

What was the biggest challenge in District 8 during your time as District Director? I consider every challenge to also present a great opportunity. A challenge during my year was the low morale and energy in District, reflecting upon lower membership. In order to reinvigorate members about the Toastmasters program and District 8, we formulated a plan of engagement with a right combination of programs and activities. Also, District has not achieved a Select Distinguished status for many years, so that was also part of challenge.

If you had a theme, what was it and what did it mean? District followed the vision of **DEEP: District Eight Enhancement Program** in alignment with Toastmasters International vision.

What was the largest success in District 8 during your time as District Director? There were many successes during year

79

2015-2016. First was District achieving "Select Distinguished status" by Toastmasters International after 9 years. District attained 45 of growth in education and training. District celebrated its 75th year anniversary as "Diamond Jubilee." District awarded "Leadership Award" to a well-known media person Don Marsh. District hosted a World Champion workshop with Mark Brown, which was well attended by TMs. District awarded Corporate Recognition award to

Washington University in Saint Louis and Express Script in Saint Louis. District formed a committee to actively develop the leadership of District, with Past District Governor Dan Darnall as chair.

On 12 Nov 2015, TI 1st VP Balraj Arunasalam presented Corporate Recognition Award to Washington University for the achievement of its two fledgling clubs—Toast of WU and WUSTL Speaks. Receiving the award was Hank Webber, Executive Vice Chancellor for Administration of Washington University in St. Louis in a ceremony at the Olin Library.

Mr. Arunasalam also presented the Corporate Recognition Award to Express Scripts for their support of seven Toastmasters clubs. Accepting the award on behalf of ESI was Mr. Mike Koehler, Vice President of Human Resources.

Special dinner with Past District 8 Governors and Mr. Balraj Arunasalam

75 years and beyond!

The past 75 years have left the Toastmasters of District 8 a long and distinguished legacy. We have persevered through war, loss, and economic ruin. We have navigated the rough waters of an ever-changing society and charted a course into a promising future. Whatever new paths we find in the years to come, the members of District 8 will continue to strive for excellence in all that we do. We have come a long way and we have a long way to go! We are leaders. We are family. We are Toastmasters.

3

CHRONICLE OF DISTRICT 8 CONFERENCES

3. CHRONICLE OF DISTRICT 8 CONFERENCES

Fall, 1985: "Homecoming." 8-9 Nov 1985, Holiday Inn North, St. Louis, MO. Conference Chair: John Mohr

Friday Night is Homecoming. Pep Rally, Skits, Cheerleading, Sock Hop.

Educational Programs (9-12am)– "Would You Like to be a Presenter" by Ken Stumpf; "The How and How Not to Elevate" by Tom Moore; "Believability Impact" by Jerry Starke, DTM, ID; "Video and You" by John Rodgers.

Table Topics Contest (1:00). The Contestmaster was Wayne Renshaw. The winners were Fred Sykes (493) (1st), Hester Owens (2nd) and Bill Grimsley (3rd).

Educational Programs Continue (4-5pm). "Putting Your Best Foot Forward" by Pat Van Noy; "How to Hold an Audience without a Rope" by Carl Miller. The conference movie was "The Art of Positive Reinforcement" by Tom Houston. Dinner & Keynote address by Jerry Starke, DTM, ID.

Humorous speech contest Contest. The winners were Tom Hornung (1229) with "The Accountant" (1st), Bill Morton with "A Funny Thing Happed to the Cemetery" (2nd) and David Summerfield with "The Hand" (3rd).

Communication and Leadership Award to Robert Blackburn of Washington University, the Director of Community and Governmental Relations and a lecturer in political sciences.

Spring, 1986: "Spring Into Action for Excellence." 30-31 May 1986, Rickman Conference Center, Jefferson City, MO. Conference Chair: Marianne Ronan.

Friday Night Dinner features Mark Twain and Tall Tales.

Educational Programs (8:45-11:30am)– "Speechcraft and Youth Leadership" by Dick Pennington; "Judging Seminar" by Tom Houston; Keynote by Ted Randall, ID; "Evaluation - Leadership Development"; "Video Self-Evaluation."

Evaluation Contest (1-2pm) The winners were Villie Appoo Koenig (1229) (1st), Dick Pennington (5573) (2nd). Dinner & Keynote by Ted

Randall, DTM, ID. International Speech contest. The winners were Herman Johnson (2389) (1st), and Ray Purvis (2nd). Distinguished Service Award to Dr. Arthur Mallory, Commissioner of Education in Jefferson, MO.

Fall, 1986: "All American Conference." 7-8 Nov 1986, Holiday Inn, Quincy, IL. Conference Chair: David Smith.

Friday Night dinner featured an All-American Ball and Tall Tales Contest. Members could dress like all-Americans. Contestmaster was Sam Geisendorfer. Contestants were Myra Morris (5318) (1st), Sherry White, Clarence Stanley, Alan Lovel (230) (2nd), and Lou Holt. Parade of Banners (8:45am).

Educational Programs (9-11:30am) – "Judging Seminar" by Gary White, DTM; "Club Management Plan" by Bill Newgent; "Leadership" by Jerry Starke, DTM ID; "Speech Evaluation" by Jim Gire; "Parliamentary Procedure" by Ted Randall, DTM.

Lunch & 20-30-40 Membership Awards. Keynote address by Verne Hagstrom, Quincy Mayor, presenting the keys to the city to Charlie Rodgers.

Table Topics Contest (1:00). The Contestmaster was Dale Fitzpatrick and the Chief Judge was Willie Summerville, DTM. The topic was "If you were president of TI, what would be your program?" The winners were John Mohr (1st), Dilip Abayasekara (2nd) and David Smith (3rd).

Business Mtg (2:00-3:30 pm). A 4-Star Architectural Tour was offered also at this time. Educational Program (3-5pm): "Leadership Development" by Dale Fitzpatrick; "The ABCs of After Dinner Speaking" by Ken Stumpf. Dinner & Keynote address by Jerry Starke, DTM, ID. Willbur receives TI Presidential Commendation.

Humorous speech contest Contest. The Contestmaster was David Smith. The winners were Tom Carr with "True Confessions of a Workaholic" (1st), John Temple with "Phone Customer Service" (2nd) and Mildred Pesante with "Car Abuse" (3rd).

Communication and Leadership Award to Leo Henning, manager of WGEM AM/FM radio.

Spring, 1987: "Carnival of the Communicators." 8-9 May 1987, Ramada Inn South, St. Louis, MO. Conference Chair: Robert Chunn, DTM.

This is an International President Visit by Ted Wood, DTM, IP.

Friday Night Dinner with carnival type food and atmosphere. Awards for best costumes and skits. White Elephant sale. Bill Treece was Chairman and Keith Woodman was Ringmaster. Skits "The Grapevine", "Guilty as Charged", "Anne and Tricky Dicky", "Song", "Good Samaritan? Smart Samaritan", The Barker's Spiel", "Coffee", "How to Tell a Funny Story."

Sat. Morning (7am) – Governor's DTM Breakfast. First time for D8 and Ted Wood, International President made the awards. Parade of Banners (8:45am).

Educational Programs (9:00-11:30am)– "Judging Seminar" by Tom Houston, "Motivating Volunteer Seminar" by Ted Wood, "Evaluation Seminar" by Ken Stumpf.

Evaluation Contest (1-2pm) The Contest master was Gary Fowler, Chief Judge was John Mohr, and the Pattern Speaker was Ellen Starke speaking on the topic "Again – Without Guilt."

Business Mtg (2:30-4 pm). Dinner & Keynote by Ted Wood, DTM, IP speaking on "Aren't You Glad".

International Speech contest master was Helyn Tharpe and the Chief Judge was Jerry Troyer.

Communication and Leadership Award to Zane Barnes, Lineman to Chairman of the Board.

"Toastmasters Are Watching" Award to Robin Smith, reporting the news on Channel 4, KMOV.

Fall, 1987: "Toastmasters Pow Wow." 6-7 Nov 1987, Days Inn, Edwardsville, IL. Conference Chair: Ruby Rodgers.

Friday Night harvest buffet dinner, parade of costumes, Tall Tales

1987 D8 Conference, Friday Night
Harry Pleis

Contest and Kahok Indian Dancers. Prentis Faw won the Tall Tales contest. Roast of Charlie Rodgers, IPDG. Educational Programs– "Media Interview Training or

Shine in the Lime Light" by Tom Kirkpatrick; "Speechcraft Panel" by Jack Rardin; "Personal Communications – The Scope of Conversation" by Sharon Schwindemann.

Table Topics Contest (1:00). The Contestmaster was Keith Woodman and the Chief Judge was Mohamed Kazi. The winners were Diane Strecfuss (1st), Robert Reilly (2nd) and Sam Gersendorfer (3rd). Dinner & Keynote address by Carl Miller (D30) ID. Humorous speech contest Contest.

1987 D8 Conference Friday Night

The Contestmaster was Bill Newgent and the Chief Judge was Dottie Carlson. The winners were Martha Ruppert (1st), Robert Duarte (2nd) and David Simmons (3rd).

Communication and Leadership Award to Karl Monroe, past publisher of the Collinsville Herald.

Spring, 1988: "The Fabulous Fifties." 20-21 May 1988, Sheraton Westport Plaza, Creve Coeur, MO. Conference Chairs: Chuck & Sally Carpenter.

Friday Night dinner, lip sync entertainment and Sock Hop. White Elephants sold at the 5&10cent store. Educational Programs– "Judging the Humorous & Table Topics Contests" by Tom Houston; "A Brief Look at The Success Leadership Programs" by Ken Stumpf; "Voice and Speech Improvement for Public Performance" by Dr. Larry Floyd.

Evaluation Contest- The Contest master was Willie Summerville and the Chief Judge was Lorraine Newgent. The Pattern Speaker was Nancy Smoot. The winners were Bill Treece (1st), Carol Warner (2nd) and Gary White (3rd). Movie by Ken Houston – "Speaking to 1 to 1000." Dinner & Keynote by Fran Weaver, DTM, ID.

International Speech contest master was Charlie Rodgers and Chief Judge was Jerry Troyer. The winners were Gary Fowler with "Silver &

Gold" (1st), Michael Lewis with "Marching to the Heart Beat of Life" (2nd) and Joe Funk with "The Real Challenge of the 1980s" (3rd).

Fall, 1988: "School Daze." 18-19 Nov 1988, Days Inn, Columbia, MO. Conference Chairs: Dottie Carlson and Tom Houston.

Early Bird Activities on Friday Afternoon – Golf, Seminars, Tours. Friday Night Tall Tales Contest, School Daze Program, Show & Tell.

Educational Programs (9-12am)– "The Art of Evaluation" by Kathryn Hille, CTM; "Your Secret Weapon – Your Voice" by Sherry White, DTM; "Who Would Want to Visit Our Town" by Jerry Preston; "The Magic of Leadership" by Al Ott, DTM; "Business Communication" by Persis Mehta, ATM; "Good

Nov. 1988 D8 Conference, Table Topics Contest
Dave Smith (DG 1989-90), Wilbur Fox 1st place (DG 1969-70), George Peo

Management" by Fran Weaver, DTM; "Public Relations at the Club Level" by Mohamed Kazi, ATM.

Table Topics Contest (1:00). The Contestmaster was Marin Blevins and the Chief Judge was Dick Weber. The winners were Wilbur Fox (1st), Tom Zimmerman (2nd) and Richard Pieper (3rd). Dinner & Keynote address by Fran Weaver, DTM, ID.

Humorous speech contest Contest. The Contestmaster was Gary White and the Chief Judge was George Peterson. The winners were John Mohr, ATM (2389) with "One's Extravagance"(1st), Harold Washington with "Culture Shock" (2nd) and Prentis Faw with "Texas IceBreaker" (3rd).

Communication and Leadership Award to Rod Gelatt, Chairman of the Broadcast News Dept. of UM-Columbia, MO.

Spring, 1989: "Capitol Speakeasy." 5-6 May 1989, Holiday Inn South, Springfield,

89

May 1989 D8 Conference
Lorraine Newgent, George Peo, John Mohr (TM of the Year)

IL. Conference Chair: Larry Aut.

Early Bird Activities on Friday Afternoon – Golf (22 members), "Building Your Thinking" (18 members), Tours (9 members). Friday Night Casino and auction. Entertainment by Lamphier High School Lion's Pride floor show.

Educational Programs– "Distinguished Club Program" by Patricia Van Noy, DTM, ID, "Dealing with Difficult People" by Jean Lebedun, Ph.D., "Contest Judging, by John Mohr, ATM, "Parliamentary Procedure" by Dick Weber.

Evaluation Contest (1-2pm) The Contest master was Kathy Hille and the Pattern Speaker was Ralph Kreigh, ATM. The winner was Marianne Ronan (Alpha) (1st), Harold Krampert (2nd) and Margaret Ranford (3rd). Dinner & Keynote by Patricia Van Noy, DTM, ID. Special presentation for Charles C. McBrian. Also, Abe Lincoln spoke to the group.

International Speech contest master was Jerry Starke (D35). The winner was Marian Guidry (Winged Word) with "From Lemons to Lemonade (1st), Gary Cummins with "Symbol of America's Freedom" (2nd) and Nate Randall with "Save the Children" (3rd).

Fall, 1989: "Show Up for the Showdown." 3-4 Nov 1989, Days Inn, Downtown, MO. Conference Chair: Kathryn Hille, CTM.

Friday Night Rendezvous. Celebrating 125 years of St. Louis history. Dinner followed by Mountain Man Storyteller, Costume Contest, Tall Tales Contest, and Skit Contest. Recognition of ATMs & roast of George Peo.

Educational Programs– "Delegate with Success" by Al Ott, DTM; "You Can Remember" by Dick Storer, DTM, PID (D30); "Increase Your Vocabulary Simply" by Myra Morris-Peo; "Publicity That Works" by Jack Rardin, DTM.

Table Topics Contest. The winners were Hubert Williams (1st), Al Ott (2nd) and Marianne Ronan (3rd). Dinner & Humorous Contest. The winners were David Grant (1st), Eric Lanham (2nd) and Stan Stimmel (3rd).

Spring, 1990: "Great Rivers Gathering." 11-12 May 1990, Holiday In, Alton, IL. Conference Chairs: Louis Smith.

Friday Night Great Rivers Gong Show. The entertainment was Dancing, singing, comedy, storytelling and skits led by Terry Warner and judges Lorraine Newgent, Nick Greles, Charlie Rogers, David Smith. Keynote by Charlie Rogers, DTM, ID.

Educational Programs (9:40-11:30am)– "Planting, Cultivating & Harvesting Your Field of Dreams" by Mike Martin, DTM; "Judging the Humorous Speech Contest" by John Mohr, ATM; "The Case of the Apple Corp TM Club" by Jon Greiner, DTM; "Introducing the Speaker and Presenting the Award" by Dick Chadwick, CTM.

Evaluation Contest (1:30-2:30pm)- The winner was Fox (1st). Dinner & Keynote Address by Patricia Van Noy, DTM, ID. Presentation of Annual Awards. International Contest. The winners were Bill Stanley (1st) and Jack Rardin (2nd).

Fall, 1990: "50 Years and We Have Just Begun." 9-10 Nov 1990, Holiday Inn, Clayton, MO. Conference Chair: Keith Woodman. 50th Anniversary coordinated by Jack Rardin, DTM.

Friday Night Entertainment. 50th Anniversary kickoff, "D8 What a Difference it Made", "Video Interview of CC McBrian", "Honor Roll of Clubs (1940-1950)", "Special Recognition to D8's 3 oldest clubs."

Clubs present skits to celebrate Smedley and the legacy of Toastmasters. Keynote – Michael Martin, DTM, ID.

Educational Programs– "Evaluation Program" by Hubert Williams, CTM; "Follow the Form" by John Mohr, ATM; "Adding Humor" by Keith Woodman, ATM; "50 Years and We Have Just Begun" by Wilbur Fox, DTM & Gary White, DTM.

Table Topics Contest. Persis Mehta was TM, Nancy Jones was Chief Judge. The winners were Tony Montgomery (FRB 4928) (1st), Mary Hose (4938) (2nd), and Rosa Fonseca (4043) (3rd).

Dinner & Humorous Contest. Richard Chadwick was TM, Al Ott was Chief Judge. The winners were Bob Winters (1229) (1st), Tony Montgomery (FRB 4928) (2nd), and Bill Treece (286) (3rd).

Nov. 1990 D8 Conference, 50-yr Celebration
Recognizing Uptown (538), chartered Oct. 1947
Mary Hose, Sherry David Smith

Nov. 1990 D8 Conference, 50-yr Celebration
Recognizing Metropolitan (348), chartered Jan. 1946
Mary Hose, Sherry White, Mike Lewis, George Noll

Nov. 1990 D8 Conference, Appreciation Certificates
Lorraine Newgent, Harry Pleis, Phil Vonder Haar, Dick Weber, Wilbur Fox, Adam Bock, Al Ott

Spring, 1991: "Jail House Rock." 17-18 May 1991, Holiday Inn Executive Center, Columbia, MO. Conference Chairs: Ralph Kriegh, ATM-S.

Dinner & Humorous Contest. Persis Mehta is TM, John Mohr is Chief Judge. Friday Night Tall Tales "I fought the Law and Law Won", "Tell it to the Judge", "The People's Court."

Educational Programs (9:40-12am)– "The Non-Verbal Agenda" by Jim Sauer, DTM; "The Dynamics of Being at Your Best" by Carolyn

Masters, DTM; "Membership Recruitment & Retention Plan" by Nancy Jones, AMT; "How to Be a Chief Judge" by John Mohr.

Evaluation Contest - Persis Mehta, DTM was TM, John Mohr, DTM was Chief Judge. The pattern speaker for the Evaluation Contest was Bob Daniels, DTM. The winner was Dan Coughlin. International Contest. Paul Lloyd, ATM was TM, Al Ott, DTM was Chief Judge. The winner was Bill Stanley. Keynote by Mike Martin, DTM, ID

Fall, 1991: "Outer Limits." 8-9 Nov 1991, Holiday Inn, St. Louis, MO. Conference Chair: Sherry White, DTM.

Friday Night: Roast of Lorraine Newgent, IPDG followed by Table Topics Contest. The winner was Frank Lloyd (Capitol), CTM. Keynote – John Griener, DTM, Region V ID.

Educational Programs (9-12 am)– "Ax or Sugar-Coated" by Al Ott; "Something New" by Lorraine Newgent; "No Free Speech" by Michael Lewis; "Judging Humorous Speech Contest" by Persis Mehta; "Successful Club Planning" by Steve Watkins; "Small Talk" by Bob Daute; "Selling Your Club" by Sally Carpenter; "Problem or Opportunity" by Ralph Kreigh; "Put Spice into your Meeting" by Lynn Williams.

Luncheon Speaker - Dick Storer, PID, "Leave The Club a Little Better than You Found It." Special Education Program – "Building Winning Speeches" by past D8 Contest Winners; "She Said, He Said" by Walt Sala, D30. Dinner Keynote – John Greiner followed by Humorous Contest. J.C. Hagan was the TM. The winner was Vonnieta Trickey. Communication & Leadership Award Recipient – Elaine Viets.

Spring, 1992: "Meet Your International President." 22-23 May 1992, Hampton Inn, Downtown St. Louis, MO. Conference Chair: Harry Pleis. This was a TI President visit by Jack Gillespie, DTM and his wife Grace.

Friday Night is Folk Lore "Virginia' Song", "TM Acronyms",

"Election Campaign Speech or the Wizzard of Uhs", "Ode to Evaluation", "TM Telephone Techniques", "The Great Duo." Evaluation Contest follows with Al Ott, DTM as TM and Howard

Citron as Chief Judge. The winner was Mehta Sizemore, CTM. Keynote (8:20-8:45) – Jack Gillespie, DTM, Int'l President.

Educational Programs (1:45-5:20pm)– "Judging TT and Eval Contests" by Persis Mehta; "Table Topics" by Kathy-Jo Facteau and Paul Kremer; "Club Officer" by Lorraine Newgent; "Public Relations: Techniques and Tools" by Sally Carpenter; "Start a New Club" by Bill Newgent; "Membership" by Max Boyko; "Speech-O-Matic: Better Speeches through Organization" by Bruce Korbesmeyer; "Speechcraft" by Floy Westermeier; "Overcome your Fears" by David Dickherber; "Keys to Success" by Eileen Hemenway and Glen Ballou.

May 1992 D8 Conference, Presidential Visit
District 8 Annual Awards
Ralph Kreig (AG of the Yeear), Jack Gillespie (Int'l President), Steve Watkins (TM of the Year)

TI President Address (1-1:30 pm) Jack Gillespie, DTM, IP. Dinner, Jack Gillespie, DTM keynote entitled "Never Stop Growing, Keep Going Up."

International Contest with Lorraine Newgent as TM and Joyce Jackson as Chief Judge. The winner was Michael Lewis (5000) (1st) and Frank Lloyd, ATM (7009) (2nd).

1992 D8 Conference, Presidential Visit
stermeier, Jack Gillespie (Int'l President), ?

Fall, 1992: 13-14 Nov 1992, Ramada Convention Center, Effingham, IL. Conference Chair: Roger Worman.

Friday Night featured square dancing.

Nov. 1992
Glen Knutson, Carol Warner

Keynote (8:45) – Jon Greiner, DTM ID or Ted Randall, DTM, PID.

Educational Programs (9:15-11:30am)– "Humor Workshop" by Keith Woodman, DTM; "Speech Ideas" by Floy Westermeier; "Parliamentary Procedure" by Dick Weber, DTM; "Creative Thinking" by Paul Kremer, ATM-B; "How to Sell Toastmasters" by Bill Treece, DTM; "Judging Seminar – Evaluation Contests" by Persis Mehta, DTM; "Evaluation Tips" by Al Ott, DTM; "Effective Meetings" by Susan Hayden, DTM; "The Club Specialist" by Ralph Kreigh, DTM.

Table Topics Contest (1:00-2:30 pm). The TM was Prentiss Faw, DTM and the chief judge was Joyce Jackson, DTM. The topic was "Rented hall for daughter's wedding. Daughter is locked in the room and will not come out. What do you do?" The winner was Kathy-Jo Facteau (1st) and Bill Treece (2nd).

Special Education Programs (4:45-5:15pm) – "So You Want to be an Area Governor" by Greg Andrus, ATM and "CTM Why?" by Lorraine Newgent, DTM.

Dinner & Humorous Contest. The TM was Al Ott, DTM and the chief judge was Joyce Jackson, CTM. The winner was Cristine West (1st), Phyllis Fisher (2nd) and Bruce Moore (3rd).

The Communication and Leadership Award was presented to Thelma Keller for her many years of service to Effingham, IL.

Spring, 1993: 30Apr-1May 1993, Kenrick Seminary, St. Louis, MO. Conference Chairs: Wesley Talcott.

Friday Night was pizza then an Evaluation Contest. The TM for the contest was Myro Morris-Peo and the chief judge was Persis Mehta. The winners were Glen Knudson (1st) and Eileen Hemenway (2nd). Next was a Stump Speech Contest.

Keynote – Jon Greiner, DTM Region V ID

Educational Programs (1:45-4pm)– "Judging TT and Eval Contests" by Persis Mehta; "Table Topics" by Kathy-Jo Facteau and Paul Kremer; "Club Officer" by Lorraine Newgent; "Public Relations: Techniques and Tools" by Sally Carpenter; "Start a New Club" by Bill Newgent; "Membership" by Max Boyko; "Speech-O-Matic: Better Speeches through Organization" by Bruce Korbesmeyer; "Speechcraft" by Floy Westermeier; "Overcome your Fears" by David Dickherber,

Special Education Program (1:45-4) "Mental Flexibility, Part I of Building your Thinking Power" by Jon Greiner, DTM, ID; "Improve Your Management Skills" by Jenny Pagano, DTM, ID.

Special Education Program (4:20-5:20) "Keys to Success" by Eileen Hemenway and Glen Ballou. Fireside chat with ID (4:05-4:15) – for current and new Area and Division Governors.

Dinner & International Speech Contest. The TM for the contest was Jerry Hoeflein and the chief judge was Joyce Jackson. The winner was John Mohr with "The Fruits of Victory" (1st), Stanley Jordan with "The Mask of an Impossible Situation" (2nd) and Fran Erickson with "I'm a Mirror" (3rd).

Fall, 1993: "Love and Marriage Celebration." 19-20 Nov 1993, Holiday Inn, Collinsville, IL. Conference Chairs: Lorraine Newgent, DTM and Lynne Williams, DTM.

Friday Golf during day, Line dancing at night followed by Tall Tales Contest. The tall tales included "The Third Edition", The Wedding That Was" by Floy Westermeier and Verlyn Tank, "Wedding Traditions" by Prentiss Faw, "Appetizers Served", "The Wedding of All Wedding" by Sam Stimmel.

Sat Morning Breakfast (7:15-8) Roast of IPDG Chuck Carpenter- "Chuck Roast." Keynote (8:30-9am) – Dick Benson, DTM Region V ID.

Educational Programs (9:15-12 am)– "Special Professional Seminar – Personality Types and Communication" by Nicholas Di Marco; "Mini-Success/Leadership Module: How to Listen Effectively" by

Michael Lewis; "Confronting Conflict Confidently" by Jenny Pagano, DTM; "Better Speaker Series" by Glen Knudson; "Serving as Chief Judge" by Persis Mehta; "Evaluation Paradigms" by Ralph Kreigh; "Toastmasters Q&A" by Richard Benson.

Table Topics Contest (1:30-2:30 pm) had John Mohr as Toastmaster with the topic: "JFK said, 'Ask not what your country can do for you, but what you can do for your country.' What can you personally do for your country?" Winners were Paul Kremer (1st), Mary hose (2nd) and Barb Grzenczyk (3rd).

Dinner &. Keynote address by Jenny Pagano, DTM, ID.

Humorous Contest had Peggy Isgrigg as TM of the contest. Paul Kremer speaking on "On the Outside Looking In" (1st), Tom Shelton with "I'm confused" (2nd) and Sally Carpenter with "The Road to Recovery" (3rd).

Communication and Leadership Award to Michael Shannon of the American Red Cross.

Spring, 1994: "Gateway to Growth." 13-14 May 1994, Holiday Inn, St. Peters, MO. Conference Chair: Jean Inabinett, DTM.

Friday Dinner is a luau by the pool. Sat morning Roast of IPDG Ted Wear. Keynote Ian Edwards, DTM TI 2nd Vice President. Educational Programs– "Low Budget Marketing – Hands-on Strategies" by Bonnie Prigge from Meramec Regional Planning Commission; "Mini-Success/Leadership Module: Characteristics of Effective Leaders" by Omer Roberts; "Judging International Speech Contests" by John Mohr; "Judging Humorous Speech Contests" by Fran Erickson; "Etiquette for Speakers" by Lisa Powell; "High Performance Leadership" by Ted Randall; "Sticks and Stones may Break my Bones" by Peggy Richardson; "Toastmasters Q&A" by Ian B. Edwards.

Evaluation Contest had Glenn Knudson as Contestmaster and Debra Smith was the Pattern Speaker. The winners were Paul Kremer (1st), Dionne Wisniewski (2nd), and Bruce Moore (3rd). Ian Edwards keynote & Int'l Contest. Winner was Jack Rardin with "Great Job Dad" (1st), Paul Kremer with "The Common Dominator" (2nd), and Carolyn Ittner with "Life's Little Miracles" (3rd). 1st year to recognize new DTMs with DTM line.

Fall, 1994: 11-12 Nov 1994, Ramada Inn & University of Missouri-Rolla. Conference Chairs: Paul Kremer, DTM and Peggy Isgrigg, DTM.

Friday Night Murder Mystery coordinated by the Rolla-Salem Community Players. Keynote – Dick Benson, DTM, Region V ID. Educational Programs– "Communication and Commitment in Everyday Life" by Patrick O'Brien; "Folklore of the Miz-Zou-Rah" by C.W. Parker; "Judging Table Topics & Eval. Contests" by Fran Erickson; "Voice Empowerment Techniques" by Carol Warner; "Storytelling: The Art of Entertaining" by Kathy-Jo Facteau; "Able Parliamentarian Program" by Sally Carpenter; "Leadership Styles" by Brian Czapinski.

The Table Topics Contest had Michael Lewis as Contestmaster with topic "How would you declare your genius?" Winners were Jerry Hoeflein (1st), Brent Stewart (2nd), Donald Lacey (3rd). Humorous Contest. Chuck Carpenter was Contestmaster and Sherry White was Chief Judge. The winners were Stephen Springmeyer speaking on "The Toastmaster's Guide to Better Driving" (1st), Mark Derby with "Rudy the All Start Reindeer" (2nd), George Noll with "Honey, Could You Do Me a Favor?" (3rd).

Communication and Leadership Award to Mayor C. Clark Leonard of Salem, MO.

Spring, 1995: "Confidence is a Choice." 19-20 May 1995, Holiday Inn, Carlinville, IL. Conference Chairs: Lynn Hawk and Nate Randall.

Friday Afternoon Golf followed by Dinner, Line Dancing and a Tall Tales Contest. Keynote – Tommy Richardson, DTM Region V PID (filling in for his late wife Peggy Richardson who died in office as ID) speaking on "Using Common Sense(s)." Educational Programs – "Using Common Sense" by Tommy Richardson, PID; "Chief Judge Seminar" by Fran Erickson; "Club Newsletter" by Chuck Carpenter; "Motivational Speaking" by Michael Lewis; "Able Parliamentarian Program" by Glenn Knudson; "Speaker to Trainer" by Paul Kremer; "Judging Hands-on Training" by Fran Erickson.

Evaluation Contest with Enjetta Fleming (Talu 9643) as Pattern Speaker with the title "The Power of Positive Doing." The winner was Rita Brigman (9903) (1st), Dionne Wisnieski (2nd), Lynne Hedrick (3rd).

Dinner & International Speech Contest. Roger Worman, DTM was Contestmaster and Peggy Isgrigg, DTM was Chief Judge. The winners were Paul Dugo (532) with "Lessons" (1st), Sgt. Robert Danbridge with "To Protect the Weak and Innocent" (2nd) and Ms. Pat Mathisa with "Commitment and Discipline in Marriage" (3rd).

Fall, 1995: "Treasure Island." 17-18 Nov 1995, Holiday Inn, St. Peters, MO. Conference Chairs: Rosia Primous.

Friday Night featured a Treasure hunt, a Scavenger hunt then a costume contest. Sat Morning Breakfast included roast of IPDG Steve Watkins. Keynote– Dick Hawley, DTM, Region V ID. Educational Programs– "Presented Speechcraft" by Marilyn Craig; "Keys to Effective Leadership" by Jean and David Inabinett; "Judges Training for Humorous & International Speech Contests" by Cindy Larm; "How to Build a Winning Speech and Other Lies" by John Mohr; "Membership Building" by Frank Pagano.

Table Topics Contest with topic "How do you make up your mind or help others to make up their minds?" The winners were Ernestine Ledbetter (1st), Roger Worman (2nd) and Joe Harpole (3rd).

Dinner & Humorous Contest. The winner was Judy Campbell with "Back in Action" (1st), Robin Hight with "Honey, Please Don't" (2nd) and Bob Deufel with "One Bird's Eye View of Almost Intelligible Writing" (3rd). Communication and Leadership Award to Penny Lorenz-Bailey who is Ms. Wheelchair for 1995-96 and has worked to prevent adolescent brain and spinal cord injuries.

Spring, 1996: 24-25 May 1996, Henry VIII, St. Louis, MO. Conference Chair: Arthur Hampton.

Friday Night fun night with Sir Arthur's Court theme. Keynote- Jenny Pagano, DTM, Region V ID with "What is TI Doing for You?"

Educational Programs– "Component Judges Seminar" by Cindy Larm, ATM; "Evaluate to Germinate Toastmasters – Grow Together" by Joyce Jackson, CTM; "Winning in Your Life and How to Win Cooperation" by Roland DeRose, DTM; "Able Parliamentarian Program" by Charles Rogers, DTM; "Membership Building Panel" by Skip Caywood; "The Art of Storytelling" by Kathy Jo Facteau; "Hands on Practice Judging" by Cindy Larm; "TI Convention" by Chuck Carpenter, DTM; "The ABC's of Leadership" by Jenny Pagono, DTM.

Evaluation Contest with Gwen Sawyer (D54) as Pattern Speaker speaking on "Pebbles – Will You Make a Difference?" The contest winners were Rachel Hassenyager (1st), Kelly Regnier (2nd) and Marilyn Lewis (3rd).

The International Speech contest winners were Michael Brundy with "Choosing Your Attitude" (1st), Paul Kremer with "Which Lens Will You Be?" (2nd) and David Koehr with "The Power of Speech" (3rd).

Fall, 1996: "Program of Stars." 22-23 Nov 1996, Holiday Inn – Viking Inn, St. Louis, MO. Conference Chairs: Carole Breckner and Dianna Jones.

Friday Night focus on Hollywood Stars which included costume contest then a screen test. Roast of Outgoing District Governor Floy Westmerier. Keynote Address - Irma Perry, DTM, ID.

Educational Programs– "Internet Cyber Surfing" by Christine Jarzenbeck; "Wild, Wild Rules of Order", Gary White (1996-97 Parliamentarian); "Teaser for Moments of Truth" by Jenny Pagano; "Get With the PROgram" by Sally Dunn (D63 LGET); "Judging Evaluations in Speech Contests" by Mary Kerwin; "Oh No, Not Another Toastmaster Meeting" by Michael Lewis.

Table Topics Contest had Contestmaster Jane Messinger with the topic "Describe Your after-dinner Thanksgiving Activity." The winners were Anne Hilchen (1st), Audrey Holman (2nd), Carol Warner (3rd). Dinner & Humorous Contest. The Humorous contest winners were Pat Mathias with "PMR- Professional Metrolink Rider" (1st), Shannon Whalen with "The Building" (2nd), Jim Nonnan with "Dr. Love" (3rd). District Communication & Leadership Award to Steve Jankowski, St. Louis radio and TV personality.

Spring, 1997: 8-10 May 1997, Capitol Plaza Inn, Jefferson City, MO. Conference Chair: Cindy Larm.

TI President Bob Barnhill, DTM, visited D8 at this conference. Friday Night was a President's costume ball. Keynote speaker was Bob Barnhill.

Educational Programs– "Chief Judge Training" by Mary Kerwin; "Have Tales – Will Travel" by Gladys Coggswell; "The 5 Ws of Club Building" by Kathy Steece, DTM; "Parliamentary Procedures II" by Gary White, DTM (96-97 Parliamentarian); "RAF-Master Building

Plan" by Rachel Hassenyager; "More Than Club Ideas" by Frank Pagano, DTM. Special Education Program- "A New Era – The Dual Track" by Robert Barnhill, DTM

Evaluation Contest. The Contestmaster was Jim Salih, ATM and Chief Judge was Lynn Hawk, STM. The pattern speaker was Pat with title "Drama of My Trauma." The contest winner was Carol Warner (4938) (1st).

Laura Mae Stewart was recognized for her 24 years of continuous support and dedication for the Alpha and Omega clubs. The International Speech Contestmaster was Ted Wear, DTM and Chief Judge was Mary Kerwin, ATM. The contest winner was Michael Brundy (1st).

Fall, 1997: "Toastmasters Outlet." 14-15 Nov 1997, Holiday Inn Wentzville, MO. Conference Chair: Joyce Jackson.

Friday Night dinner. The Table Topics Contest Chief Judge was Kay Brainerd, CTM. The winner was Dan Malan (1st). Saturday Breakfast - Roast of Outgoing District Governor James Schwarz. Keynote Address– Frank Pagano, DTM, ID.

Educational Programs - "What's the Difference" by Jean Inabinett; "Arm Swinging, Ugly Faces and Other Things" by Jack Langston, DTM; "Judging an Evaluation Contest" by Kay Brainerd; "Beyond the Club – Area Governor" by Shash Bhave; "A Tour Through 'American'" by Jane Messenger, ATM; "Judging an International Contest" by Kay Brainerd; "Toastmasters Shopping List 101 – TI Catalog"; "Extra, Extra – Club Newsletter"; "Parliamentary Procedure" by Sherry White, DTM, PDG.

The Humorous contest winner was Nate Randall with "Toothpaste" (1st) per D8 V17#2 & D8 Award booklet at Fall 98 conference; however, Paul Dugo is cited incorrectly as winning in D8 V18#1. District Communication & Leadership Award to Otis Woodward, St. Louis radio personality.

Spring, 1998: "Spring Into Toastmasters." 15-6 May 1998, Hampton Inn, Downtown, St. Louis, MO. Conference Chair: Jim Salih, ATM.

Friday Night dinner then Evaluation Contest (8:30pm). The contest winner was Kelly Regnier (1st). Keynote speaker was Irma Perry, DTM, ID.

Educational Programs– "Parliamentary Procedure – The Practical" by Sherry White, DTM; "What's My Motivation for Self-Improvement" by Irma Perry, DTM, ID; "Creativity 101" by Joe Taylor; "If You Have a Minute, Judging Table Topics" by Kay Brainerd; "Toastmasters with much Conviction" by Floy Westermeier, DTM; "Leaders are Like Eagles - They Don't Fly in Flocks" by Ana Anita Atok; "A Funny Thing Happened on my Way to the Contest – Judging Humorous Speech" by Kay Brainerd; "Contest Discussion" by Angell Chisholm; "Club Newsletters."

Dinner & International Contest. The Contestmaster was Michael Lewis and the Chief Judge was Kay Brainerd. The International Speech contest winner was Joe High (1st), Rick Neuber (2nd) and Dale Sunderman (3rd).

Fall, 1998: "Little Speech on the Prairie." 20-21 Nov 1998, Holiday Inn, Decatur, IL. Conference Chairs: Leslie Waddell and Dallas Hixson.

Friday Night dinner theme is "School Daze." Table Topics Contest followed at 9pm with Gary White, DTM as Contestmaster. The Table Topics winner was Lynda Espinosa (Fairview Hts) (1st), Denia Fields (Heart of Missouri) (2nd), Felicia Cotton (Plan Employees) (3rd).

Saturday Breakfast - Roast of Outgoing District Governor Jean Inabinett, DTM. Keynote Address (9am) – Floy Westermeier, DTM, ID.

Educational Programs– "International Speech Judging" by (no presenter listed); "Chief Judge" and "Evaluation Contest Judging" by Angell Chisholm, ATM-G; "Speak with More Energy" by Rick Neuber, ATM; "Think Better, Listen Better, Speak Better, But Let's Have Fun at It" by Victor Costa, ATM; "Gavel Talk" by Steve Watkins, DTM; "A Recipe for Perfect Toast" by Cheryl Norsic, CTM; "Fish Bat and Burlap: A Toastmaster's Guide to New Ideas" by Joe Taylor; "Fun Raising" by Floy Westermeier, DTM.

Dinner & Humorous Contest. The Humorous contest winners were John Mohr (2389) (1st), Lynda Espinosa (Fairview Hts) (2nd) and Judy Campbell (FRB) (3rd).

District Communication & Leadership Award to Gregory Freeman.

Spring, 1999: "Spring Fling." 21-22 May 1999, Ramada Inn-Six Flags, Eureka, MO.

Friday Night dinner then Evaluation Contest (8:30pm). The contest winners were Vanessa Goodwin (1st), Debbie VanHorn (2nd), Sonya Matzig (3rd). Keynote speaker was Floy Westermeier, DTM, ID. Educational Programs- "The New Distinguished Club Plan" by Floy Westermeier, DTM; "Transforming Your Past into D8's Future" by Darrell Grimes, DTM; "Who's on First?" by Oliva Ly-Pieknik, ATM; "Judging Session" by Angell Chisholm; "Leadership with a Higher Standard" by Ruth Newsome, DTM; "Dynamic Mentoring" by Richard Chadwick, DTM.

Dinner & International Contest. The Contestmaster was James Schwarz, DTM and the Chief Judge was Angell Chisholm, DTM. The International Speech contest winners were Joe High with "It's Just Not Fair" (1st), Don Hawley "The Wall" (2nd) and Rick Neuber with "Would You Take a Chance?" (3rd).

Fall, 1999: "Celebrate TI 75th Anniversary." 5-6 Nov 1999, Holiday Inn, Collinsville, IL. Conference Chair: Tom Coscia.

Friday Night Hors d'oeurves, Fun Night by the Meramec Improvisational Group presenting improve skits about Dating Game, Mansion on the Hill, Unlikely Super Heroes, Alphabet Story, Freeze on the Moon. Table Topics contests follows with the topic: "The Holidays are just around the corner, so families everywhere will be celebrating in their own traditional way, tell us about your favorite family tradition, why is it your favorite?" The winner was Elaine Laura (1st).

Roast of Ed Rowold, immediate past DG. Keynote – Ruth Newsome, DTM, ID with "Not Distinguished?"

Educational Programs – "Humorous Speech Judging" by Angell Chisholm, DTM; "Perfecting the Art of Evaluation" by Debbie Van Horn; "Small Group Dynamics" by Sherry White, DTM; "Table Topics Judging" by Angell Chisholm, DTM; "How to Run a Quality Meeting" by Eric Tryon, CTM; "How Networking Works for Toastmasters" by Marcia Griffin (Bank of America); "Giving and Taking at Table Topics" by Anita Washington-Harding; "Club Mentoring and Beyond" by Ruth Newsome; "Public Relations" by Kathy Cissell. Humorous Contest. The winner was Mary Ann Paille (1st). Communication and Leadership Award to Dr. Deborah Dee. She

Nov 1999 D8 Fall Conference
Table Topics Winners

Nov 1999 D8 Fall Conference
Humorous Contest Winners

is the Commissioner on the Disabled for St. Louis City.

Spring, 2000: "Motivating for the Millennium." 19-20 May 2000, Westport Comfort Inn, Maryland Heights, MO. Conference Chair: Wayne Allen.

Friday Night Hors doeuvres, entertainment was volunteers trying to win $20. The pattern speaker for the Evaluation Contest was Elaine Tilman. The winner was Rachel Hasenyager (1st).

Sat. Morning Breakfast – Roast of Carole Breckner, outgoing DG.

Educational Programs – "How to Judge a Contest" by Angell Chisholm, DTM; "Parliamentary Procedures" by Sherry White, DTM; "Creating a Speech is Easy" by Debbie Van Horn; "Chief Judge vs Contest Chair" by Angell Chisholm, DTM; "Tips for Taming Table Topics" by Barbara Shelton, ATM-S; "Membership Building" by Floy Westmeier, DTM,ID; "Websites and Their Effects" by Kathy Cissell, ATM-S & Dennis Beard, ATM-B; "How to Have a Successful Corporate Club" by Dick Chadwick, DTM; "Speaking to Motivate" by Barbara Reynolds, ATM-B.

May 2000 D8 Spring Conference
Evaluation Contest Winners
Mary Ann Paille (3rd), Michael Lewis (2nd), Rachel Hasenyager(1st)

May 2000 D8 Spring Conference
International Speech Contest Winners
Denia Fields (3rd), Cheryl Norsic (2nd), Kelly Regnier (1st)

Dinner & International Contest. The winner was Kelly Standing-Regnier (1st).

Fall, 2000: "Celebrate District 8's 60th Birthday." 10-11 Nov 2000, Best Western, Columbia, MO. Conference Chairs: Tanya Clatterbuck, ATM, Amy Bexten, DTM, Carole Breckner, DTM.

Friday Night Birthday Party Games included a Pinata, Pin the Tail on the Toastmaster, cakewalk, decorations, balloons and a birthday cake. Festivities were followed by Table Topics Contest. The topic was "What 1900's decade would they like to visit?" Cathy Babis selected 1950's music and placed first.

Roast of Outgoing District Governor Carole Breckner. Keynote – Chuck Carpenter, DTM with "What is in it for me?"

Educational Programs– "Rebuilding a Club" by Dick Chadwick, DTM; "Goal Setting" by Ernie Lowden, DTM; "Quality Club Meetings" by Wayne Allen, ATM; "Starting a Club" by Dick Chadwick, DTM; "Storytelling" by Barbara Shelton, ATM; "Effective Table Topics and Evaluation" by Michael Lewis.

Jon Greiner announced his candidacy for 3rd VP. Chuck Carpenter announced his candidacy for Region V ID. David Shanahan was confirmed as Div. A Governor. Dinner & Humorous Contest. Ann Noonan won the Humorous Speech Contest with "Facts of Life."

Communication and Leadership presented to Bob Priddy, new director of Missourinet, a statewide commercial radio network of about 70 stations.

Spring, 2001: "Happy Birthday, D8." 18-19 May 2001, Keller Ramada Inn & Conference Center, Effingham, IL. Conference Chairs: Mary Kerwin and Roger Worman.

Friday Night Hors d'oeuvres and Trivia. Winners were Carole Breckner, Mary Hose, Teresa Shell, and several first timers. Evaluation Contest followed. The pattern speaker was Sid Williams, on "Why Hitler Lost WWII." The winners were Steve Watkins (1st), Charles Danganan (2nd) and Harry Sneed III (3rd).

Keynote – Justin Gottfried, DTM, Region V ID. Educational Programs– "International Director Panel" by Floy Westermeier, DTM and Justin Gottfried, DTM; "Parliamentary Procedures" by Sherry White; "How to Bring Fun in the Club"; "How to Conduct Contests" by Angell Chisholm; "How to Be an Effective Leader"; "How to Be a New Club Mentor" by Dick Chadwick, DTM.

Dinner & International Contest. The winners were Kelly Standing-Regnier with "A Smile for Every Raindrop" (1st), Wesley Andrues (2nd) and Dan Malan (3rd).

Fall, 2001: "A Taste of St. Louis." 16-17 Nov 2001, Radisson, downtown St. Louis, MO. Conference Chair: Wes Talcott, ATM-S.

Friday Night is a formal banquet with etiquette points. Table Topics Contest followed and the winner was Mary Buchanan (1st). Saturday Breakfast - Roast of Outgoing District Governor Cindy Larm. Keynote – Justin Gottfried, DTM, ID.

Educational Programs – "Rebuilding Your Existing Club" by Dick Chadwick; "The Well-Gestured Speech" by Denia Fields; "First-Timer Orientation" by Tom Coscia; "Judges Training Workshop" by Carole Breckner; "A Toastmaster Wears Many Hats" by Chuck Carpenter; "New Club Development" by Dick Chadwick. Dinner & Humorous Contest. The winner was Sandy Albrizzi (1st).

Spring, 2002: "Partnership Along the River of Toastmasters." 17-18 May 2002, Pere Marquette Park, IL. Conference Chair: Alison Baker.

Friday Night American Indian Dance presentation. Evaluation Contest followed and the winner was Ellen White (1st). Saturday Keynote – Chuck Carpenter, DTM, ID.

Educational Programs– "Toastmasters in the Workplace" by Chuck Carpenter, DTM; "Forum: Sound Off on District Conference" by Joe Passanise, ATM-S; "Who Moved My Cheese" by Sandra Swearingen, ATM-S; "Using Visual Aids for Dynamic Presentation" by Michael Warner; "Customer Service – What's in a New Member" by Floy Westermeier, DTM, PID; "Video Conferencing" by Ollie Richards; "Where Do We Go From Here" by Millie Fortune-Gilpin, ATM-B.

Dinner & International Contest. The winner was Samson Burrell (1st).

Fall, 2002: "Magic of the Best." 15-16 Nov 2002, Holiday Inn Southwest & Viking Center, Crestwood, MO.

Friday Night was Night of Magic with John Sonnenshein. Table Topics Contest followed with Carolyn "Carol" Buening (4492) winning the contest. Saturday Breakfast - Roast of Outgoing District Governor Shash Bhave.

Educational Programs– "Contest Judging Seminar" by Michael Stewart; "Speech Contest Planning" by Michael Stewart; "Basics of

Parliamentary Procedures" by Joe Passanise; "New Club Sponsorship" by Nancy Jones.

Dinner & Humorous Contest. The Int'l contest winner was Lois Ann Marler (1056) with a speech entitled "Life with a Tightwad." District Communication & Leadership Award to Thomas Tener, VP from Martiz.

Spring, 2003: "Building Toward Your Best." 30-31 May 2003, University of Missouri-Rolla, MO. Conference Chairs: David Mallory, ATM and Cindy Larm, DTM.

Friday Night was Dinner, followed by the Evaluation Contest. The winner was Barbara Hunt (1st).

Keynote speaker was Chuck Carpenter, DTM, ID. Dinner & International Contest. The winner was Matthew McCready (1st).

Fall, 2003: 14-15 Nov 2003, Airport Hilton, St. Louis, MO.

Friday Night had a Trivia Night followed by the Table Topics Contest. The topic was "Who do you feel has made the most interesting or important discovery and why?" The winners were Bob Glidewell (1st), Dawn Tucker (2nd), Dan Darnall (3rd). Roast of Outgoing District Governor Omer Roberts. Keynote Address – Joan Diehl, DTM ID.

Educational Programs– "Connecting with Your Audience" by Nancy Boyle; "The Importance of Service" by Sally Carpenter; "Not Just for New Clubs" by Terry Rolan; "Starting a Website" by Dan Jones; "What Do I Do Now (First Aid)" by Chief Robert Hardy III; "Peak Performance", by Ivan Paul. Dinner & Humorous Contest. The Humorous contest winners were Wayne Allen (1st), Brian Day (2nd), Sid Moore (3rd).

Spring, 2004: "Building Toward Your Best." May 2004.

Friday Night included dinner and a fun night coordinated by Solae Toastmasters (606012). Evaluation Contest followed with Sharon Scott-Moyer as pattern speaker. The winner was Dan Darnall (1st). Keynote speaker was Nancy Jones, DTM.

Educational Programs– "Distinctions Between Coaching & Mentoring" by Tony Gartner; "Dress for Success" by Sharon Scott-

Moyer; "Dual TM Tracks and the Leadership Paradigm" by Robert Gergen; "Best Practices" by Kevin Desrosiers and Rosemary Wilson; "Train the Trainer – Specific to TLI" by Nancy Jones; "Personal and Business Etiquette" by Carol Warner. Dinner & International Contest. The Winner was Rolondo Berry (1st).

Fall, 2004: 8-9 Nov 2004, Airport Hilton, St. Louis, MO. Conference Chair: Ed Rowold. TI President Jon Greiner, DTM, visited D8 at this conference.

Friday Night "Family Feud" based on questions about Jon Greiner's life. The Table Topic topic was: "What animal would best depict the kind of person you are?" The Table Topics winner was Yolandea Wood who picked a cuddly teddy bear.

Roast of Outgoing District Governor George Noll. Keynote Address – Jon Greiner, DTM, Int'l President. Educational Programs– "S.U.C.C.E.S.S." by Johnny Campbell and Tony Powell. Carole Breckner declared her candidacy for Region V ID. Dinner & Humorous Contest. The Humorous contest winner was Tom Carr (1st) with a speech entitled How to Fix Your Fear Factor". Steve Hughes was 2nd and Mark Johnson was 3rd.

Spring, 2005: 20-21 May 2005, Northfield Inn and Conference Center, Springfield, IL. Conference Chairs: Larry Aut and Catherine Key.

Friday Night included dinner and Trivia night conducted by Carol Warner. Evaluation Contest with Bob Gergen taking 1st. Keynote speaker was Lonn Pressnall as Abraham Lincoln. Dick Poirer, ID, talked on the proposed duess increase to be voted on at TI in August.

Educational Programs– "Attract and Retain New Members" by Sandra Swierenga; "Sharpen Your Silver Tongue" by Barbara Kryvko; "Judges Training" by Dale Lancaster; "Parliamentary Procedure" by Jackie Monroe.

Dinner & International Contest. Ranjeet Singh placed first in the Int'l speech contest, Rolando Berry was second and Dawn Tucker was third.

Fall, 2005: "Make a Splash at the Fountains at Fairview." 18-19 Nov

2005 May D8 Conference
Officer Installation
Dan Darnall, Michael Lewis, Dick Poirer, Nancy Jones, Mary Kerwin, Barbara Kryvko, Pamela Wickman

2005,

Sheraton Four Points, Fairview Heights, IL. Conference Chairs: Michael and Carol Warner, DTM.

Jim Key, 2003 World Champion Public Speaking, attended the conference. The Table Topics winner was Nate Randal, with Jane Clark second and Michael Hopkins third.

Saturday Breakfast - Roast of Outgoing District Governor Nancy Jones. Keynote Address – Stephanie Weiss, DTM (Past Area 9 Gov.) speaking on "Three Coins in a Fountain." Special Educational Session – Charles Albright, DTM, ID speaking on "Increasing Membership/Club Coaches."

Educational Programs– "Effective Evaluations – a Panel of Past Champions" led by Bob Gergen, DTM; "Life and the Lemonade Stand" by Nancy Holth and Diana Weiss; "Hitting the Mark: The Quest for Excellence" by Jim Key. Dinner & Humorous Contest. The

Humorous contest winner was Marlyn Whitney (1st), Steve Hughes was 2nd and Dawn Boyer was 3rd.

Humorous Speech Contest

Second place winner Steve Hughes with Dan Darnall, Barbara Kryvko and Mary Kerwin. ↓

↑ Contest winner Marlyn Whitney with Dan Darnall, Barbara Kryvko and Mary Kerwin.

↑ Third place winner Dawn Boyer with Dan Darnall, Barbara Kryvko and Mary Kerwin.

Table Topics Contest

Second place winner Jane Clark with Mary Kerwin and Dan Darnall. ↓

↑ Contest winner Nate Randall with Mary Kerwin and Dan Darnall.

↑ Third place winner Michael Hopkins with Mary Kerwin and Dan Darnall.

May 2006 D8 Conference
Evaluation & International Contest Winner
Mary Kerwin, DTM (DG); Dan Darnall, DTM (LGET); Sade Tago, ATM-B
(winner); Barb Kryvko, DTM (LGM)

Spring, 2006: "All the Trials to Excellence." 19-20 May 2006, Stoney Creek Inn, Columbia, MO. Conference Chairs: Carol and Jerry Buening.

Friday Night BBQ. Evaluation Contest with Sade Tagbo taking 1st. Keynote speaker was Cathy Salter, Columbia Tribune Columnist and National Geographic author.

Educational Programs- "Letting the World Know about Toastmasters" by Dick Poirer, ID; "Contest Judging 101" by Joe Passanise, DTM; "Creating a Club Website" by Andria Wallace; "Tales of Boon's Lick" by Ralph Kreigh, DTM; "Put the WOW Back into Your Meetings" by Kevin Desrosiers, ATM-S; "You're So Funny" by Marlyn Whitney; "Grip & Grin" by Mag Langland.

Special Educational Programs – "Building Your Leadership Power: Characteristics of Effective Leaders" by Tom Houston. Dinner & International Contest. Sade Tagbo placed first in the Int'l speech contest.

Fall, 2006: 17-18 Nov 2006, Millennium Hotel, Downtown St. Louis, MO. Darren LaCroix, 2001 World Champion Public Speaking, attended the conference.

Friday Night Beach party and Luau. The Table Topics winner was David Poland, with Kevin Desrosiers second and Linda Spall third.

Saturday Breakfast - Roast of Outgoing District Governor Nancy Jones. Special Educational Session – Charles Albright, DTM, ID speaking on "Increasing Membership/Club Coaches."

Educational Programs– "From Chump to Champ" by Darren LaCroix, DTM. Dinner & Humorous Contest. The Humorous contest winner was Bob Marx (MAC Toastmasters) (1st), Bob Glidewell (Mid Mo Advanced Club) was 2nd and John Mohr, DTM (2389) was 3rd.

Spring, 2007: "All the Trials to Excellence." 11-12 May 2007, Doubletree, Chesterfield, MO.

Friday Night BBQ. Evaluation Contest with Robert Gergen taking 1st. Educational Programs– "Youth Leadership," "Improving Your Speeches Using Audio & Video," "How to Organize Contests," "Voice Coaching," "How to have a Successful Club," "The History of Ralph Smedley," "How to Turn Your Humorous Speech into a

Contest Winner." Dinner & International Contest. Jill Kennedy-Broughton placed first in the Int'l speech contest.

Fall, 2007: 30 Nov-1Dec 2007, Decatur Conference Center & Hotel, Decatur, IL.

Edward Hearn, 2006 World Champion Public Speaking, attended the conference. Col. Jill Morganthaler, 2-time D30 Winner, fought Saddam Hussein in Iraq and used impromptu speaking to deal with a mob in Bosnia.

Friday Night is the Big Easy Buffet. The Table Topics winner was John Baranzelli. Saturday Breakfast - Roast of Outgoing District Governor Dan Darnall.

Educational Session– "Effective Evaluations by Understanding Personality Styles" by Chuck and Rachel Alt; "Power Point: Four Critical Ideas" by Capt. Nils French; "Understanding Judging Forms for Better Judging" by Jerry and Cindy Hoeflein; "How to Create Videos – Toastmasters & TV: The Perfect Combo" by David Lisnek.

Dinner & Humorous Contest. The Humorous contest winner was John Murphy (1st).

Spring, 2008: "Aim for Perfection, Settle for Excellence." 9-10 May 2008, Holiday Inn, St. Peters, MO. Keynote: Richard Avdoian of National Speakers Association with "Team Work by Design." Keynote: Sharon Scott-Moyer with "Leadership and Communication – Is There a Link?"

Evaluation Contest with Kevin Desrosiers taking 1st. Educational Programs – "Mastering Impromptu Speaking and Table Topics" by David Lisnek; "Set Up a Club Website" by David Lisnek; "Be a Club Coach" by Mike Raffety; "Personal Development" by Richard Avdoian; "Communications in a Flat World" by Nancy Holth; "Contest Briefing" by Jerry and Cindy Hoeflein. Dinner & International Contest – Winner was John Baranzelli (51).

Fall, 2008: "Celebr8 Success." Nov. 2008, Holiday Inn, South County, MO. The Keynote speaker was Lethia Owens who talked on developing a personal brand. The Table Topics topic was "If you win this contest tonight, we are going to give you a million dollars. What is

112

the first thing you are going to do with the money?" The winners were Jerry Hoeflein (1st), Kevin Desrosiers (2nd), Dawn Tucker (3rd).

Roast of Outgoing DG Barbara Kryvko. Keynote Address by Mike Raffety, DTM, ID - "The Courage to Conquer." Ed Session – "Staying Distinguished with the Distinguished Club Plan," "The Do's and Don'ts of Contest Judging," "Speech Writing Made Easy," "Leading from the Lectern: Self Coaching Tools to Help You Kick Your Fear to the Curb," "Evaluate to Win." The Humorous contest winners were John Barry with "Brief" (1st), Jeffery Williams (2nd), Phillip Mueller (3rd).

Spring, 2009: 15-16 May 2009, Truman Hotel, Jefferson City, MO. Conference Chairs: Sharon Silva and David Mallory. Keynote: Michael Smith, DTM, ID "Time for Change." Friday Night started with a reverse Toastmasters meeting. Evaluation Contest followed with Jef Williams taking 1st.

Educational Programs – "The Attitudes of a Winning Team" by Dr. Stephanie Houseman; "Discovering Your Memory Powers" by Jay Grosfield; "Presentation Technology" by Charles Hunter; "Is There Life Beyond CC? The Advanced Manuals" by Tom Coscia, STM; "The Best Lollipop on the Block - Speechcraft" by Nancy Jones; "Component Leadership Manual" by Margaret Walker. Dinner & International Contest. – The International Speech contest winner was John Mohr, DTM, who asked the audience to find and follow a vision in their lives.

Fall, 2009: "Motiv-8 Today to Cre-8 a Better Tomorrow." 20-21 Nov. 2009, Crowne Plaza, Clayton, MO.

Friday Night is dinner with a Tall Tales presentation by the Wry Toastmasters. The Crossroads Toastmasters club sang "Toastmasters in the Sky." The Table Topics topic was "Address Congress to Designate the Turkey as the National Bird." The winners were Jerry Hoeflein (1st), Chris Robinson (2nd), Terry Rolan (3rd).

Saturday Breakfast - Roast of Outgoing District Governor Tony Gartner. Students from a Toastmasters Youth Leadership Program sponsored by St. Clair Club present the colors. Educational Session (1-4 pm) – "The Key to Effective Evaluations," "Advanced Speech Writing Made Easy," "The CL Manuals and Beyond," "What Makes a Successful Club," "Serving as a Club Officer," "Toastmasters and Social Networking Through the Web."

The Humorous contest winners were Margaret Walker (1st), Polansky (2nd), Mark Mahan (3rd).

Spring, 2010: "The Road to Your Destiny Begins on Route 66." 7-8 May 2010, Route 66 Hotel and Conference Center, Springfield, IL.

Friday Night sock hop with Matthew Stevens DJ. Evaluation Contest followed with John Murphy taking 1st, David Mallory taking 2nd and Bob Gergen taking 3rd. Educational Programs – "Stress Management," "Topic Research," "Developing Dynamic Agendas." The International Speech contest winners were Jef Williams (1st), Ramesh Chandrani (3rd).

Fall, 2010: "A Funny Thing Happened on the Way to the Lectern." 12-13 Nov. 2010, Harrah's Casino and Conference Center.

Friday Night is dinner with an Improv presentation by Improv Trick. The Table Topics topic was "River." The winner was Jerry Hoeflein (1st).

114

Roast of Outgoing District Governor Dori Drummond. Keynote Address was provided by John Baranzelli, author of *Making Government Great Again* and member of McBrian Lincoln-Douglas Toastmasters, who presented about the importance of Toastmasters in our lives.

D8 Communication and Leadership Award to Sam Silverstein, 2009 Keynote at TI Convention. His presentation stressed accountability.

Ed Sessions – "Accountability and Personal Leadership" by Sam Silverstein; "Advanced Techniques for a Successful Seminar" by Gary Hebert; "How Fun is It?" by Dawn Tucker; "You Can't Push Wet Spaghetti!" by John Murphy; "010 Job Market Forecast: Cloudy"; "Toastmasters and Social Networking Through the Web." Dinner & Humorous Contest. The Humorous contest winner was Brenda Knight from River City Toastmasters.

Spring, 2011: "Toastmasters Together – One World." 29-30 April 2011, Crowne Plaza, Downtown St. Louis, MO. Conference Chair: Carole Breckner.

George Yen, International 2nd Vice President attended from Taiwan.

Friday Night celebrated the cultures of the world. Evaluation Contest followed with Carrie Radnov speaking on: "Are You Interesting?" The winners were Kevin Desrosiers (1st) and Margaret Walker (2nd).

Keynote by George Yen on how we can achieve greatness together.

Educational Programs – "How to Serve as a Long Distance Mentor," "How to do the High Performance Leadership Module," "Making Your Toastmasters Club Multi-Culturally Friendly," "Practical Parliamentary Procedure," "Using Social Media to Enhance Your Business Communication," "Sounding Good in English."

Dinner & International Contest. The International Speech contest winner was Arnita Jones and Alan Kirby was second.

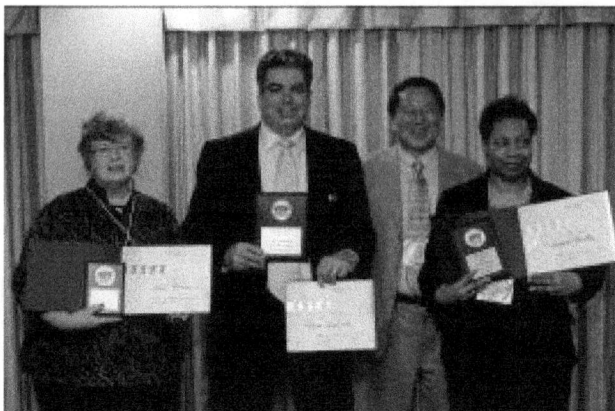

Fall, 2011: "Wild Wild West." 18-19 Nov. 2011, Capitol Plaza Hotel, Jefferson City, MO. Conference Chair: Cynthia Scroggins.

Darren LaCroix Workshop on Thursday, 17 Nov. at the Florissant Library. Darren won the 2001 World Championship of Public Speaking. Friday Night is dinner Square Dancing. The winner was Raymond Allen (1st), Debbie Hyde (2nd), Dori Drummond (3rd).

Roast of Outgoing District Governor Tim Spezia. Keynote Address was provided by Croix Sather on "100 Marathons, 100 Keynotes & 100 Dates."

Educational Session – "Dream Big, Act Big – Unleash the Superstar Within" by Croix Sather; "New TI Brand"; "Social

Networking"; "Club Coaching"; "New Free Toast Host" by Tim Spezia and Lora Mather; "District Trio and District Roles" by the Top 3.

Dinner & Humorous Contest. The Humorous contest winner was John Baranzelli (1st), John Barry (2nd). Brandon Brown (3rd).

Communication and Leadership Award to Paul Pepper, a Columbia, MO longtime TV and radio host.

Spring, 2012: "Leap Into Success." 18-19 May 2012, Holiday Inn at Six Flags, Eureka, MO. Conference Chairs: Jacquie Vick and Jef Williams.

Keynote by Rebecca Bennett. Friday Night celebrated as Mardi Gras theme with live jazz and a surprise scavenger hunt.

Evaluation Contest followed with Mark Strothmann as pattern speaker. The winners were Tom Huling (1st) Jeremy Epperson (2nd) and Erin Gissel (3rd).

Educational Programs– "Become a Star Player on an All-Star Team (Leadership-Followership," "Motivation to Grown," "Public Speaking for Visibility and Profit (Panel Discussion," "Secret to Giving Rave Reviews (Evaluations)," "Speaking Power," "Tribal Leadership: Finding and Building New Leaders."

Andrew Little, ID, presented a keynote at lunch.

Dinner & International Contest. The International Speech contest winner was Tom Huling (1st), Damon Watson (2nd) and Alan Kirby (3rd).

Fall, 2012: "Forging Active Lifelong Learning." 16-17 Nov. 2012, Pere Marquette Lodge, IL. Conference Chairs: Taffy Cobb or Yolandea Wood.

Friday Night is the Lodge's famous chicken dinner with Clue Murder mystery of Mr. Toastbody. The winner was Raymond Allen

(1st). Saturday Breakfast - Roast of Outgoing District Governor Tom Coscia. Keynote Address was provided by Robert M. Dandridge.

Educational Session – "Write Your Next Speech" by Don Clare; "Give a Great Table Topics Answer" by Jerry Hoeflein & Wayne Allen; "Practice Table Topics" by John Bohning; "Give an Effective Evaluation" by Erin Gissel & Adam Kutell; "Paint Word Pictures" by Carrie Radnov; "Build Your Club and Retain Members" by Dietmar Wagenknecht, ID, Sandy Kardis, Bridgette Wesley, and Ray Allen; "Go From Speaker to Trainer" by Becka Clark; "Craft That Contest Winner Speech" by Tim Huling, John Mohr, and Jef Williams; "Know Your Toastmasters Practices and Protocol" by Dori Drummond, Mary Kerwin and Tom Coscia; "Communicate Effectively in Different Cultures" by Robert Danbridge.

Dinner & Humorous Contest. The Humorous contest winner was Chandan Unchageri (1st).

Communication and Leadership Award to Michelle Tucker, vice chair for the United Way Community Impact Committee.

Spring, 2013: "Classic Hollywood – 1930s and Beyond." 17-18 May 2013, Renaissance Hotel, St. Louis, MO. Conference Chair: Wendy Clothier.

Friday Night was Hollywood night with many stars. The Evaluation contest winners were Thomas Huling (1st), Raymond Allen (2nd), Kathleen Arnold (3rd). Keynote by Cathy Newton challenged us to live in full swing by flexing our risk-taking muscles.

Educational Programs– "Lights, Camera, Action! Anatomy of a Humorous Speech," "Motivation to Grown," "The Table Topics Award Goes to...," "Set the Stage: How to Have a Successful

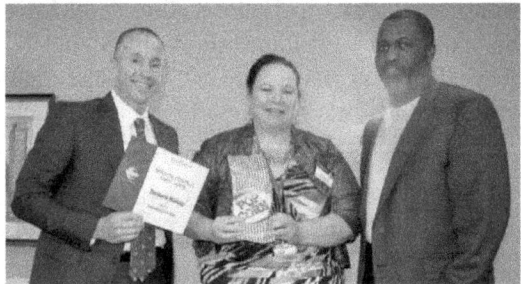

Toastmasters Meeting," "A Star is Born ...You!," "Fill Those Seats," "Leading District 8," "Your Path to Stardom," "Mock Contest: Casting Call and Roll Credits," "Critics Corner: Evaluating the Performance," "Go From Starlet to Star with Social Media."

Dinner & International Contest. – The International Speech contest winner was Matt Prose (1st), David Evans (2nd) and Valerie Rasche (3rd).

Fall, 2013: "Celebrating Milestones on a Toastmasters Journey." 22-23 Nov. 2013, Union Stations, Downtown St. Louis, MO. Conference Chairs: Rachel Francis and Richard Porter.

The Table Topics contest winner was Kevin Desrosiers (1st). Keynote Address Friday night was provided by Tom Dowd speaking on "Transformation Time with Transformation Tom."

Roast of Outgoing District Governor Curtis Scroggins. Awards Presentation of education and leadership and membership awards and recognition of new DTMs.

Dinner & Humorous Contest. The Humorous contest winner was David Kincade (1st).

Spring, 2014: "A Toastmasters Chautauqua – Leaving a Legacy Through Leadership." 2-3 May 2014, Capitol Plaza Hotel, Jefferson City, MO. Conference Chairs: Ralph Kreigh and Leigh Britt.

Friday Night celebrated as a Chautauqua from the late 1800s and early 1900s. Evaluation Contest followed with Mrs. Gopinath as pattern speaker. The winners were Dan Darnall (1st), Raymond Allen (2nd) and Neva Nicols (3rd). Keynote by Tony Richard. Tony is founder and senior partner of Clear Vision Development Group.

Educational Programs– "The 5 W's of Writing, Publishing and How" by Becky Michael; "Ready, Set, Go! Get Your Social Media Campaign Up and Running" by Genevieve Howard.

Special Ed Program - Revitalized Education Program" by Bob Gergen.

Dinner & International Contest. – The International Speech contest winner was Sudharshan Anandan (1st), Alan Kirby (2nd) and David Kincade (3rd).

Fall, 2014: "Toastmaster's Anthology Celebrating 90 years of Advancement." 14-15 Nov. 2014, Collinsville, IL. Conference Chair: Tom Gillard.

Friday Night Dinner. The Table Topics contest winner was Frank

Laviola (1st). Keynote Address was provided by Jef Williams.

Saturday Breakfast - Roast of Outgoing District Governor Lora Mather.

Dinner & Humorous Contest. The Humorous contest winner was Lemont Curry (1st).

Spring, 2015: "Cultures around the World." 29-30 May 2015, Sheraton Westport Plaza Hotel, St. Louis, MO. Conference Chair: Lisa Cooksey-Cannon.

Friday Night presented a Fashion Show from around the world.

Evaluation Contest followed. The winner was Valerie Rasch (1st). Keynote by Rebecca Clark speaking on "The Power of Words!" Dinner & International Contest. – The International Speech contest winner was Tawanna Watson (1st).

Fall, 2015: "Diamond Jubilee of District 8, Learning, Growing, Leading." 13-14 Nov. 2015, Double Tree Hotel, Chesterfield, MO. Conference Chair: Vickie Calmese.

Friday Night Dinner with the D8 Got Talent Review. The Table Topics contest winner was Ron Heif (1st). Keynote Address was provided by TI 1st Vice President Balraj Arunasalam speaking on "Change Yourself To Change The World."

Educational Programs - "Talk Tech Better," "Social Media & How to Use LinkedIn," "Sharpening Your Chops," "The Code to Greatness," "Bringing Your Dreams to Reality—Vision Boards," "Connecting—More than Words," "Drive: 5 Elements of Leadership" by Balraj Arunasalam, DTM; "Mindful Leadership."

Roast of Outgoing District Governor Sandra Kardis. Dinner & Humorous Contest. The Humorous contest winner was Vamsi Jammalamadaka (1st).

Spring, 2016: "District 8—Taking the Lead - Yesterday, Today and Tomorrow." 6-7 May 2016, Sheraton Clayton Hotel, St. Louis, MO. Conference Chair: Joann York, DTM.

Friday Night will have a Division Feud with dinner.

Evaluation Contest followed, with Dhanuja Singh placing 1st. Educational Programs– "7 Elements of a Winning Story" by John Barry; "The Inspiring and Engaging with Effective Feedback" by Don Carter; "Your Speaking Voice" by Margaret Walker; "Body Language of a Good Listener" by Jef Williams; "Making a Positive Impression" by Brian Catanzaro; "Prezi – Presentations that get Noticed" by Brian Jones.

International Contest - The International Speech contest winner was Dhanuja Singh (1st). Dinner Contest. Comedy and improv with special guests the "No Confetti Allowed Improv Players," Mike McGuire and George Haynes.

4

NOTEWORTHY

4. NOTEWORTHY

Oldest 8 in District 8

Distinctive - Oldest clubs active in the District as of 2016:

McBrian Lincoln-Douglas Club (51)	Springfield, IL
Midtown Clayton Toastmasters Club (283)	Clayton, MO
Webster Groves Toastmasters Club (461)	Webster Groves, MO
Fort Leonard Wood Club (493)	Ft. Leonard Wood, MO
St. Clair Club (496)	Belleville, IL
Capital Club (503)	Jefferson City, MO
Tarsus Toastmasters (532)	St. Louis, MO
O'Fallon Toastmasters (994)	O'Fallon, IL

Twelve (12) Women District Leaders of District 8 in 75 years!

Special recognition to the women who have served in the District's highest office, in an organization that long banned women from membership:

Lorraine Newgent, DTM	District Governor 1990-1991
Floy Westermeier, DTM, PID	District Governor 1995-1996
Jean Inabinett, DTM	District Governor 1997-1998
Carole Breckner, DTM	District Governor 1999-2000
Cindy Larm, DTM	District Governor 2000-2001
Nancy Jones, DTM	District Governor 2004-2005
Mary Kerwin, DTM	District Governor 2005-2006
Barbara Kryvko, DTM	District Governor 2007-2008
Dori Drummond, DTM	District Governor 2009-2010
Lora Mather, DTM	District Governor 2013-2014
	District Director 2016-2017
Sandy Kardis, DTM	District Governor 2014-2015

Farzana Chohan, DTM   District Director 2015-2016

2016: Select Distinguished District 8 – 3rd time in 75 years

District 8 was recognized by Toastmasters International as a Select Distinguished District most recently for the 2015-2016 TM year.

District Director Farzana Chohan recounts her sentiments about the accomplishment:

It was an honor to receive a "Select Distinguished District" Award for District 8 by Toastmasters International President Jim Kokochi at the 85th convention in Washington, D.C. As the flashlights from cameras, iPhones, and iPads created a surreal feeling, so does the attention of over 1000 pairs of eyes in the audience. It is a humbling experience to stand on a stage so huge - the stage which has accommodated over 140 people with flags of countries at the opening ceremony. As I reflect upon the leadership journey, to me it is clear that District 8 has achieved this award dues to the hard work of each member of this District, club officers and team work. It was not possible without the support of each member who has worked on their education and leadership goals and submitted them to TI to move to next level of growth. The selfless dedication to develop skills and grow while helping fellow Toastmasters is the core element for our District's success.

The "Hall of Fame" ceremony on Thursday night was full of fellow Toastmasters from all around the world. District 8 had thirteen members attending the convention. We had made a 19-foot-long banner to walk on the stage and I am happy to report to you that we received many accolades for the size and branding of our banner. D8

group looked very sharp as they presented District 8 on stage and received the award.

On Friday afternoon, at the Golden Gavel event, leaders of successful Districts were presented to convention attendees. The event planner lined up everyone behind the stage in a narrow, relatively dark aisle, where you can see TRIOs in front of you and behind you, while you can also see them walking on stage on the backside of a big screen, hanging above your head. And, of course, you are talking to your cohorts from other districts while waiting for your turn to go on stage. This little experience reminded me of the leadership journey, where you can see in front and behind and to future on the horizon, when everything is not clearly visible, but the sense that you are on a right path with your intuition and vision as guiding lights.

As Kat and I walk up into flashing lights of all types of cameras, it was an amazing moment. We raised our hands together and validated the work of each member of our District. The energy in the crowd was electrifying as the delegates were full of camaraderie and the spirit of Toastmasters.

When many of my non-Toastmasters friends asked me what kind of monetary reward this award brings, the answer is simple: the bond, the experience, learning and growing are above and beyond any monetary gains. Knowing each one of you, my fellow Toastmasters, is PRICELESS!

5

LIFELONG UNDERTAKINGS

5. LIFELONG UNDERTAKINGS

This is the list of District 8 members, who joined Toastmasters in 1970s and 80s and have continually maintained their paid membership. This list is derived from Toastmasters International membership on 3/31/2017.

Join Date	First Name	Last Name	Club Name
2/1/72	William	Meyer	High-Noon Toastmasters
9/1/73	Vernon	Boeckmann	O'Fallon Toastmasters, Fairview Heights Toastmasters Club
10/1/73	John	Mohr	Aerospace Orators
1/1/74	Gary	White	Jeffco Challengers Club, Aerospace Orators
11/3/74	Sherry	White	Jeffco Challengers Club
10/1/75	Howard	Brandt	South County Toastmasters
2/1/79	Sandra	Swearingen	O'Fallon Toastmasters
12/1/79	George	Myers	McBrian Lincoln-Douglas Club
7/1/80	Carl	Hendrickson	South County Toastmasters
9/1/80	Tom	Zimmerman	Anheuser-Busch Toastmasters
6/1/81	Dale	Fitzpatrick	Effingham Toastmasters
6/1/81	Thomas	Ahillen	Anheuser-Busch Toastmasters Club, Open Line Toastmasters
7/1/81	Charles	Carpenter	Creve Coeur Toastmasters
9/1/81	H. R.	Pennington	Waynesville-St. Robert Area Toastmasters
10/1/81	Lance	Richter	O'Fallon Toastmasters
12/1/81	Norman	Horine	Waynesville-St. Robert Area Toastmasters
10/1/82	Thomas	Krauska	South County Toastmasters
11/1/82	Jane	Abbott Morris	Grand Center Club
11/1/82	Rosetta	Keeton	Grand Center Club
12/1/82	John	Blattner	High-Noon Toastmasters Club

2/1/83	Thomas	Cox	Grand Center Club
3/1/83	Dottie	Carlson	Columbia Toastmasters, Talu Toastmasters Club
4/1/83	Jack	Bettag	South County Toastmasters
10/1/83	Brent	Stewart	South County Toastmasters
10/1/83	Vernell	Sams	Grand Center Club
4/1/84	Lynne	Williams	O'Fallon Toastmasters, Fairview Heights Toastmasters Club
12/1/84	Bill	Burlison	High-Noon Toastmasters
12/1/84	Michal	P-Burlison	High-Noon Toastmasters
4/1/85	Shipra	Somani	McBrian Lincoln-Douglas Club
4/1/85	Benedict	Kemper	Alpha Toastmasters
4/1/85	Ronald	Drake	Grand Center Club
11/1/85	Clemente	Perez	Fort Leonard Wood Club
4/1/86	Joseph	Eulberg	Anheuser-Busch Toastmasters
4/1/86	Alan	Raymond	Midtown Clayton Toastmasters
7/1/86	Ellen	White	Grand Center Club
10/1/86	Ralph	Kreigh	Columbia Toastmasters, Downtown Toastmasters
10/1/86	Brent	Watson	Open Line Toastmasters
12/1/86	Nathaniel	Randall	McBrian Lincoln-Douglas Club,Noontime Toastmasters, Horace Mann Toastmasters
6/1/87	Sidney	Moore	Capital T Toastmasters - An Advanced Club, Webster Groves Toastmasters Club
9/1/87	Lorraine	Newgent	Fairview Heights Toastmasters
11/1/87	Danny	Moore	Anheuser-Busch Toastmasters
6/1/88	Kenneth	Freeman	Columbia Toastmasters
8/1/88	Evelyn	Horine	Waynesville-St. Robert Area Toastmasters
10/1/88	Margaret	Baggett	Lincoln University Toastmasters

John Mohr
Boeing Aerospace Orators Club (2389)
Member since 1973
2009-   Winner District 8 International Speech Contest
1998-   Winner District 8 Humorous Speech Contest
1992-   Runner-up Region V International Speech Contest
1992-   Winner District 8 International Speech Contest
1989-   Runner-up Region V Humorous Speech Contest
1988-   Winner District 8 Humorous Speech Contest
1986-   Winner District 8 Table Topics Contest
1983-   Winner District 8 Evaluation Contest

John Mohr grew up in South Dakota. He graduated from the South Dakota School of Mines and Technology in 1956 with a degree in Electrical Engineering. He also has a Master of Science degree in Electrical Engineering from St. Louis University, received in 1962. John married Alice Mohr (nee Hammond) in 1959. They have three children and five grandchildren.

After graduating from college in 1956, John came to work in St. Louis for McDonnell Aircraft Company, which later became McDonnell Douglas Corporation and now is Boeing. He retired in 1992 after 36.5 years in the aircraft industry.

John joined Toastmasters International in 1973 and is currently active in the Boeing Aerospace Orators Club (2389). He is a Distinguished Toastmaster and was District 8 Toastmaster of the Year in 1989. He has competed in many contests and with significant success.

John's Toastmasters Journey in his own words:
Once upon a time, I was a shy young freshman in college. I developed a crush on an older woman. She must have been at least 20! She was a leader in Methodist Youth Fellowship. So I joined Methodist Youth Fellowship just to be near her. This one-sided love affair ended before she found out about it! It ended because one Sunday night she came to me and said, "John, will you please prepare and present the

133

program next Sunday night?" ... I left and I never went back because I could not force myself to stand up in front of a group and talk.

This is the story of how I overcame my shyness. I became an engineer. I worked with numbers. I worked with things. I never stood up in front of people to talk! This went on for 13 years out at what is now the Boeing Company in St. Louis. It ended abruptly one day when my many-times-removed manager called a meeting and announced, "The Admiral is coming next month to learn about our program." Then he went around the room making speaking assignments and I relaxed.

Suddenly, he stopped, he stared at me, and he said, "And Mohr, you will talk about this." It is not an exaggeration to say that I saw my career flash before my eyes. With sudden clarity, I realized I had two choices: I could say, "Yes, sir." Or I could say, "I resign!" A wife and three small children tempered my decision. With false courage, I said, "Yes sir! I can do it!"

Then I began a month of frantic preparation. It was draft the viewgraphs; rehearse the viewgraphs; dry run the viewgraphs in front of the big cheese. Then go back and do it all again. The turmoil in my tummy was terrible. Perhaps you have heard the antacid commercial, "Are you having a Malox moment?" Forget about it. I had a Malox month!

At last, the dreaded day arrived. We were in a big conference room. The Admiral and his associates were in the front row. Corporate Vice Presidents were in the second row. My many-times-removed manager and his ilk were in the third row. Way in the back of the room, I sat chug-a-lugging Malox! At last, I was introduced. I strode to the front, stepped up on the podium, and moved over behind the lectern.

With trembling fingers, I punched the button to signal for the first view graph. And I gave my presentation. Wonder of wonders - I actually survived. And my reward was... more speaking opportunities! They were all the same: frantic preparation, endless rehearsal, mountains of Malox!

It all came to a head one day out at Kirtland Air Force Base. My marketer introduced me; I strode to the front; I stepped behind the lectern and my mind went absolutely, totally blank! I committed a presenter's no-no. I turned my back on the audience and stared at the screen. I stared for what seemed like an eternity before I got an inspiration. I turned back to the audience and said, "I don't remember a single thing I wanted to say about the viewgraph. So, I am going on to number 2."

That is the incident that forced me to admit that I had to have help with a speaking career that I didn't want. That is what forced me to join Toastmasters, where I knew I could get help. Has Toastmasters actually helped me? To illustrate, I will share three short events.

The first event occurred before I joined Toastmasters. The lay leader at church called and asked me to present the sermon on laity Sunday. I did everything except use the "H" word as I told him where to go. The second event occurred a couple of years after I joined Toastmasters. A new lay leader asked me to present the sermon on laity Sunday. I said, "No problem." I selected a topic, I researched, biblically and otherwise. Then, on the appointed day, I stepped into the pulpit and delivered a 20-minute sermon. The third event occurred later, when I was working in an advanced manual preparing a 20-minute inspirational speech. Suddenly, I said to myself, "This would better if presented as a sermon!" So, I called the lay leader and volunteered!

There has been a remarkable transformation in my speaking career. It is a transformation that began the day I joined Toastmasters International. It is a transformation that continues even today. Because I am still trying to get better!

When I joined Toastmasters International, there were about as many women in my club as there were in my engineering classes in the 1950's - one! Maybe Rose doesn't count because she was an engineer too. She sat next to me and inquired about Toastmasters. I invited her to join. She might have joined without being invited, because Rose was a feminist and the president of the local National Organization of Women. I'll share some thoughts about how women have impacted Toastmasters and me.

Rose had a significant impact on me with one of her early speeches, entitled, "Do You Want Your Daughter to Grow up Handicapped?" She shared her struggles of getting accepted as an engineering student in the late 1960's. The struggles for equality in the workplace were equally challenging. With two small daughters, I vowed to help them in their chosen fields. My older daughter chose Civil Engineering. Laura now works in Abu Dhabi as Director of Rails for the planning stage of the light rail system that Abu Dhabi is going to have. My younger daughter is an Industrial Engineer with a Master's degree in Environmental Engineering. Sara works for Conoco-Phillips in Alaska. After two years on the North Slope she now works in the planning for future oil field developments. Both are Registered Professional Engineers. (I say that looks good on my retirement resume.)

In days before there many women in Toastmasters, Club, Area and, Division Contests were typically dinner meetings and were well attended by men and women. For example, more than 80 men and women attended the Area 3 contest that I chaired in 1975. Men brought their wives, who were anxious for a night out without cooking. My wife, Alice, used to attend many events. But, for many years now, she only attends if I am competing. Women as Toastmasters already have a night out. It seems women are not as well supported by their husbands as we once were by our wives.

Women have a major impact on the Toastmasters organization. From being a rarity 40 years ago, women now comprise about half of the membership. This year, our top three District officers are all women. Women are active at all levels. A fringe benefit is that this provides me with the opportunity to be friends with many younger women (of course, at this point in my life they are all younger). I won't name any names. But, if you greet me with a hug the next time I see you, you are definitely one of my friends.

I also claim many men as Toastmaster friends. At the top of the list is Gary White. We have shared pizza and beer after Toastmaster meetings for more than 30 years. Beyond that, I helped get Gary elected as Lt. Governor of Administration (as it was known in the 1980's). He was out of town on company business, so I gave his nomination speech. In those days, elections were contested. Gary won by one vote on the third ballot! Gary rewarded me by designating me as District Contest Chair.

The educational aspect has changed significantly. My old basic Toastmaster manual had 15 speeches. My old advanced manual also had 15 speeches. And, that was it! Now we start with 10 speeches in the Competent Communicator manual. Next, we choose from a wide assortment of advanced manuals with five speeches dedicated the same area of expertise. All manuals (then and now) operate on the same principal: here are objectives; now go build a speech to meet those objectives. I tell people that meeting speech objectives helps to build skills.

Toastmasters has changed over the years, but the basic objective is still to help men and women to become better than they were yesterday. It works! But it doesn't come free. Improvement will be in proportion to the effort we invest in trying to improve!

Gary White

Past District Governor
District 8 Historian
Member since 1974
Boeing Aerospace Orators Club

Gary's Toastmasters Journey in his own words:

As a teenager, I started with Toastmasters by attending contests with my father who was a Toastmaster. We would discuss and evaluate the speakers and determine where the speakers could have improved and what strengths they possessed.

When I started in college I realized how helpful public speaking would be and attending a Speechcraft held by a local club. The club was composed of half community members and half from the college. I held several offices and working on progressing through the basic manual. One day we had a visitor who said he was our "Area Governor", whoever that was. Evidently we were a part of an Area and the rest of the clubs were in Houston. We attended several Area contests and then became aware of something called a "District Conference". Myself and another club member drove to a District Conference in San Antonio and experienced educational sessions and attended a Contest.

When I graduated college and moved to St. Louis to begin working, I wondered if I had to start a club in order to have Toastmasters in St. Louis. It turned out that McDonnell Douglas had 2 clubs I could join and I chose the McDonnell Douglas 2389 club. I wanted to develop my leadership skills and served in several clubs offices up to club president. The club was active in Area 3 and it was wonderful to have neighboring clubs close and not having to drive an hour to an Area contest. I competed in Speech Contests and was enjoying developing speaking skills which was useful at work when I needed to make

137

technical presentations. I then decided I wanted to become an Area Governor, but I could not since there was a tradition that the District Governor would appoint the outgoing president of another Area 3 club as Area Governor. It took a year, but I worked with the District Governor to establish a method to elect an Area Governor.

I won the sequent election and become the next Area 3 Governor. I was finding the leadership skills I was developing in Toastmasters was also transferring to the workplace. The Area Governor was an opportunity to work with a group of club presidents and we did have an active Area Council which primarily focused on planning the Area Contests. The contests were dinner events with turnouts in the 100-125 range and many members bringing their spouses. Both events were a nice dinner out and a fun evening. Being an Area Governor meant I was a member of the District Executive Committee and became aware of the activities beyond the club. I learned about planning District Conferences, forming new clubs and methods to build membership of current clubs. The Area Governorship is one of the greatest offices since you can directly impact the development of each of your clubs. I also learned about how to effectively work with people and the how the different personality types could work for the same objectives but in different ways.

When I decided I want to continue working at the District level I also learned about how to campaign. All through high school and college I hated parties, now I had to go out and work to get people to vote for me. In the early 1980s in District 8 many of the Division Governor races were contested and the Administrative Lt. Governor was always contested. I was elected as Division B (Mo. No.) Lt. Governor and learned about how to work with Area Governors to work with their clubs.

When I ran for Administrative Lt. Governor I was in a field of 4 candidates. I came in third that year and served as a Committee Chair. This gave me an opportunity learn more about the district. The next year when I ran for Administrative Lt. Governor I was in a field of 3 candidates. On the next to last ballot I tied with the other candidate. I lost the next ballot by a single vote. Therefore, the next year I again served as a Committee Chair. This was a very interesting year since we started strong with new clubs which put the district in a strong position at the halfway point. When the points were totaled, D8 had a shot at being a President's Distinguished District. We spent the next six months doing everything we could to bring new clubs in, get educational accomplishments registered and retain club membership. We were successful and did achieve Presidential Distinguished District for that year. As that year was wrapping up, I again ran for Administrative Lt. Governor in a field of 3, but had to travel for business that weekend. John Mohr handled my campaigning at the Conference and I recorded my campaign speech which John played at the lunch Stump Speech event. During the vote I once again tied with another candidate but this time went ahead by 1 vote on the final ballot.

The year as Administrative Lt. Governor provided great leadership development experience. One duty of the ALG was to prepare the District Resource Manual. This was before the advent of personal computers, so the complete roster of District Officers, Committee Chairs, and all 6 club officers had to be typed by hand. But this task, performed both in the Fall and Spring, gave me a great understanding of all club officers in the district and good insight into personnel throughout the district. This was also the time when I met an interesting Toastmaster at the International Convention who became a great friend as I learned about how to be effective in the District Leadership.

The next year I became the Educational Lt. Governor and worked to enhance the educational programs. The district election process was a disruptive event since the Educational Lt. Gov. did not advance to District Governor since a Toastmaster who ran for District Governor without moving through the senior offices defeated him. This became a lesson in how to achieve objectives through political upheaval. One change we achieved was to rearrange the District contests so that the Fall would be the Humorous Speech and Table Topics and the Spring would be the International Speech and the Evaluation. Contest judging was also a topic of discussion and how to improve it. We started to have Judging Training sessions at the District Conference.

When I was elected District Governor I strove to establish more stability in the District and worked to establish a good foundation. The focus was on developing Area Governors and helping them to develop their management abilities. We worked to get new Toastmasters into activities above the club by involving them in Area contests and District Conferences. This was successful since the District was distinguished for the first time in three years. But the foundation was laid since the District was distinguished for the next two years. This was also the first time that the District First Lady, Sherry Sala, went from fiancé to spouse during the Governor's year. Sherry also learned from her time as District Governor that you needed to keep people fed during meetings. All the meetings of the Division and Senior Officers between the Executive Committee meetings were held at the Governor's house and fed by the first lady. This was also the first year to have a Christmas party for the Executive Committee hosted by the Governor.

As past District Governor I wanted to help maintain the history of the district and became Assistant Historian under Wilber Fox. We worked together until his death in the mid 1990s when I assumed the Historian duties. The office has been very interesting since I have come to understand that accomplishments are not single events but part of a tapestry which extends into the past. Also, it is interesting to see how philosophies and concepts actually play out as they move from initial discussions to initial implantation and then how they affect the future. Looking into the documentation has shown the life and death of clubs. Looking over many years you can appreciate the creativity of members as they try new ideas and refine old ones. During the early years of my Toastmasters experience we were free to create new contests, training sessions such as for judging, and new committee chairs and new approaches to conferences. Toastmasters International has imposed many more limits on what District's can do and what contests they can hold; but it is amazing the creativity within those limits.

As a past District Governor I had the opportunity to be the Regional Conference Chair. This was a great way to learn how to put on an event for Toastmasters from many states, all from Region 5 clubs.

Lance Richter

O'Fallon Toastmasters Club (994)

Member since 1969

As per Lance's account, he originally joined Toastmasters in February of 1969 for what he calls "social reasons." A friend who was a member had been bugging him to attend, and he finally relented and attended a meeting. After seeing the program, he figured the experience would be kind of enjoyable. He says, "I joined and that was the beginning." He describes his time in Toastmasters as a good experience, and particularly a good learning experience. "I was a pretty crude young man," he recalls. "A young farm boy. I feel that I've changed quite a bit." Lance says that his tenure in Toastmasters has made him an educator, and he has strong feelings about the program and its benefits. "It's something that anyone can make use of." He is most proud of his DTM award, not because of what it meant for him, but because he realizes the importance of it as setting an example for other members.

Vern Boeckmann

O'Fallon Toastmasters (994)

Member since 1973

Vern initially joined because of a coworker's wife, who was a Toastmaster. "She saw that I got a C in speech in college, and she suggested that I join Toastmasters." It has since become one of the central activities of his life. When asked to describe his proudest achievement, Vern replied: "The look of the newbie Toastmaster when they get the confidence to stand up and look their audience in the eyes, as they smile and they know they've really accomplished something in their own mind – and I've been able to help them do that."

Louis Smith

O'Fallon Toastmasters Club (994)

Member since 1983

1988- Division Director of the Year

Louis first joined Toastmasters around September of 1983, after a member took him to lunch at a meeting of the Scott Toastmasters Club (1382). His experience has been very positive, having learned to speak up despite his natural soft voice. He is most proud any time he earns the Best Table Topics ribbon.

6

DISTRICT 8: HALL OF FAME

6. DISTRICT 8: HALL OF FAME

Toastmaster of the Year

2016	Parasarum Ananthram	1992	Steve Watkins
2015	Frank Yates	1991	Ralph Kreigh
2014	Jerry Chapman	1990	Richard Chadwick
2013	Mike Kotur	1989	John Mohr
2012	Kathryn Mokriakow	1988	Darline Lewis
2011	Jeanette Lynch	1987	Mohamed Alim Kazi
2010	Joann York	1986	Bill Newgent
2009	Dan Darnall	1985	Bob Chunn
2008	Margaret Walker	1984	Adam Bock
2007	Kevin Desrosiers	1983	George Peo
2006	Dawn Tucker	1982	Phil Vonder Haar
2005	Robert Gergen	1981	Howard Brandt
2004	Carol Warner	1980	Clifford Shahl
2003	Terry Rolan	1979	Diane Reave
2002	Carole Breckner	1978	Eugene Tesreau
2001	Joyce Jackson	1977	W. B. Finufit
2000	Angell Chisholm	1976	Wilbur Fox
1999	Charles Rodgers	1975	H. Mack Stewart
1998	Floy Westermeier	1974	J. Leo Wissbaum
1997	Lorraine Newgent	1973	Van Psimits
1996	Mary Kerwin	1972	Clarence Fultz
1995	Paul Kremer	1971	Forest Nelson
1994	Michael Lewis	1970	Harold Proffitt
1993	Mary Hose		

Division Director of the Year

2016	Bridgette Wesley		1999	Shash Bhave
2015	Tom Gillard		1998	Angell Chisholm
2014	Howard Price		1997	Cindy Larm
2013	Jeanette Lynch		1996	Edwin Rowold
2012	Deborah Morissey		1995	Joyce Jackson
2011	Lora Mather		1994	James Schwarz
2010	Kathryn Mokriakow		1993	Floy Westermeier
	Curtis Scroggins		1992	Greg Andrus
2009	Curtis Scroggins		1991	Bob Dargue
2008	Dawn Tucker		1990	Persis Mehta
2007	Sue Harrington		1989	Nick Greles
2006	Kevin Desrosiers		1988	Louis Smith
2005	Tony Gartner		1987	Jerry Troyer
2004	Robert Gergen		1986	David Smith
2003	Michael Lewis		1985	Calvin Jackson
2002	Cheryl Passanise		1984	Jack Rardin
2001	Dick Chadwick		1983	Dick Weber
	Dori Drummond			

Area Director of the Year

2016	Don Smith		1991	Greg Andres
2015	Lisa Cooksey-Cannon		1990	Charles Carpenter
	Lorie Kaplan			
2014	Tom Gillard		1989	Ralph Kreigh
2013	Taffy Cobb		1988	Ron Snider
2012	Peggy Willoughby		1987	George Peterson
2011	Debra Morissey		1986	Jerry Troyer
2010	Raymond Allen		1985	Lois Maddox
	Dossie "D.J." Randle		1984	Peggy Isgrigg
2009	Kathryn Mokriakow		1983	Tom Moore
2008	Sly Brooks			Dick Pennington
2007	Cindy Hoeflein		1982	Jack Rardin
	Dawn Tucker		1981	Gary White
2006	Bernadine Chapman		1980	Harold Friebig
2005	Sharon Scott Meyer		1979	Gene Collins
2004	Terry Rolan		1978	Harry Pleis
2003	Janet Harmon		1977	Robert Clark
2002	Michael Lewis		1976	Frank Hirt
2001	David Mallory		1975	Clifford Schahl
2000	Richard Chadwick		1974	William McQuire
1999	Cheryl Norsic		1973	Gilbert Moorman
1998	Dori Drummond		1972	Paul Altire
1997	Angell Chisholm		1971	Tom Dillon
1996	Anton Vanterpool II		1970	Joseph Seidel
1995	Cindy Larm		1969	Leroy Holiday
	Ed Rowold		1968	Richard Guignard
1994	Mary Kerwin		1967	Ross Poppenphol
1993	James Schwarz		1966	Robert Downey
1992	Floy Westermeier			
	Virginia Bolton			

Corporate Recognitions

2015 – 2016 Express Scripts and Washington University

2014 – 2015 Mallinckrodt Pharmaceuticals

2013 – 2014 Wells Fargo Advisors

2012 – 2013 Mastercard and Save-A-Lot

2011 – 2012 Enterprise and Maritz

Retired Toastmaster of the Year

2015	Chuck Carpenter and John Mohr
2014	Ralph Morissey
2013	Carole Breckner
2012	Sandra Kardis
2011	John Barry
2010	Bob Blattman
2007	Mary Kerwin
2006	Nancy Jones
2005	Lorraine Newgent
2003	Ken Oster
2002	Joe Passanise

District Speech Contest 1st place Winners

International		Humorous	
2016	Dhanuja Singh	2016	Rich Puskarich
2015	Tawanna Watson	2015	Vamsi Jammalamadaka
2014	Sudharshan Anandan	2014	Lemont Curry
2013	Matthew Prose	2013	David Kincade
2012	Tom Huling	2012	Chandan Unchageri
2011	Arnita Jones	2011	John Baranzelli
2010	Jef Williams	2010	Brenda Knight
2009	John Mohr	2009	Margaret Walker
2008	John Baranzelli	2008	John Barry
2007	Jill Broughton	2007	John Murphy
2006	Sade Tagbo	2006	Bob Marx
2005	Ranjeet Singh	2005	Marlyn Whitney
2004	Rolando Berry	2004	Tom Carr
2003	Matthew McCready	2003	Wayne Allen
2002	Samson Burrell	2002	Lois Ann Marler
2001	Kelly Regnier	2001	Sandy Abrizzi
2000	Kelly Regnier	2000	Ann Noonan
1999	Joe High	1999	Mary Ann Paille
1998	Joe High	1998	John Mohr
1997	Michael Brundy	1997	Nate Randall
1996	Michael Brundy	1996	Pat Mathias
1995	Paul Dugo	1995	Judy Campbell
1994	Jack Rardin	1994	Steve Springmeyer
1993	John Mohr	1993	Paul Kremer
1992	Michael Lewis	1992	Cristine West
1991	William Stanley	1991	Vonnieta Trickey
1990	William Stanley	1990	Bob Winters
1989	Marian Guidry	1989	David Grand
1988	Gary Fowler	1988	John Mohr
		1987	Martha Tupert
		1986	Tom Carr
		1985	Tom Hornung
		1984	Joyce Hinze
		1983	Ernest Morganegg
		1982	Helen Tharpe

Table Topics		Evaluation	
2016	Erin Gissell	2016	Dhanuja Singh
2015	Ron Helf	2015	Valerie Rasche
2014	Frank Laviola	2014	Dan Darnall
2013	Kevin Desrosiers	2013	Tom Huling
2012	Raymond Allen	2012	Tom Huling
2011	Raymond Allen	2011	Kevin Desrosiers
2010	Jerry Hoeflein	2010	John Murphy
2009	Jerry Hoeflein	2009	Jef Williams
2008	Jerry Hoeflein	2008	Kevin Desrosiers
2007	John Baranzelli	2007	Robert Gergen
2006	David Poland	2006	Sade Tagbo
2005	Nate Randall	2005	Robert Gergen
2004	Yolandea Wood	2004	Dan Darnall
2003	Bob Glidewell	2003	Barbara Hunt
2002	Carol Buening	2002	Ellen White
2001	Mary Buchanan	2001	Steve Watkins
2000	Kathy Babis	2000	Rachel Hasenyager
1999	Elaine Laura	1999	Vanessa Goodwin
1998	Lynda Espinosa	1998	Kelly Regnier
1997	Dan Malan	1997	Carol Warner
1996	Anne Hilchen	1996	Rachel Hasenyager
1995	Ernestine Ledbetter	1995	Rita Brigman
1994	Gerald Hoeflein	1994	Paul Kremer
1993	Paul Kremer	1993	Glenn Knudson
1992	Kathy-Jo Gacteau	1992	Metha Sizemore
1991	Frank Lloyd	1991	Dan Coughlin
1990	Tony Montgomery	1990	Wilbur Fox
1989	Hubert Williams	1989	Marianne Ronan
1988	John Mohr	1983	John Mohr

7

PICTOGRAPH

District 8 Governors/Directors

"Meet Me In St. Louis"

The group shown in the picture represents the committee activity in our Convention City. These men are hard at work on plans to make Toastmasters welcome next August. Their work will be wasted if great numbers of us do not accept their invitation.

This picture was taken on the occasion of Ted Blanding's recent visit to help with pre-convention details. In the front row, Blanding is shown with Director B. H. Mann, Jr., and "Andy" Anderson. In the back row we have Roland Rapp, Fritz Meek, Morris Landau, of the St. Louis Convention Bureau, District Governor William Bautema, Jack Wilder, Sales Manager of the Statler Hotel, Oscar Hollenberg, and Wendell Stark; all of them keen on making the 1949 convention the best one yet.

Program Plans

Details are being worked out by the Convention Program Committee, of which Past President J. P. Riswert is chairman, for days of intensive education and inspiration. These plans wait for final approval at the January meeting of the Board of Directors.

The Convention is dated for August 11 to 14. The first day is training time for district and international officers. Educational and business affairs will be crowded into Friday and Saturday, the 12th and 13th. Friday evening and Saturday afternoon and evening will be filled with attractive features, for the benefit of local Toastmasters.

One innovation puts the Speech Contest Finals on Saturday night, following the installation of officers, the culminating point of the Convention. Other important features will feature Saturday afternoon's session.

"St. Louis is a fine convention city, and Toastmasters are good convention glowers. So you are warned to 'Meet me in St. Louis' in August, 1949.

JANUARY 1949   21

Metamorphosis

8

NOTES

Note from Farzana Chohan

When I started, I had no idea what I was getting into!

Yes, this is exactly the same sentiment which Eileen Murphy has expressed in her note. The difference is that for me it started many years before her - to be exact almost 4 years ago! I was of the same impression that it should be a document to be done in few months; I never imagined that it would take this long. A few months have turned into a few years! Now it does make a logical sense that what I learned from a dedicated historian of District 8, who also is a Past District Governor and many more Past District Governors, would have not been captured in few months time! The chats at district and International events were the best venues to learn stories from Mary Kerwin, Floy Westermeier, Lance, Vern, John Mohr, Chuck Carpenter and fellow Toastmasters, which could have not been learned anywhere else! The richness of information and knowing that our district had played a meaningful role in development of a global organization is worth knowing!

The question I had been asked over the period of that four years is, "Why do you want to document the History of District 8?"

I don't have an answer, but I have a sentiment, which I would like to share with readers:

"Since joining District 8, I had heard the stories about long associations of people with each other and with the organization - the metamorphosis of personal and professional lives, linked together through District 8 Toastmasters.

The information I encountered was intriguing, but, in the beginning, I was not able to appreciate the magnitude of history in the first few years as a novice member. Once I started seeing my own metamorphosis along with others who started with me, I began to get a real grasp on the impact it had throughout its history on humans! The uniqueness that it is not a spiritual or political entity and is relatively inclusive was definitely a plus. The gender barrier from the early days of the organization of barring women are now removed, opening it up for women participation around the world.

Thus, when Lora asked me to be Public Relations Officer for the District, I agreed. As a PRO, I wanted to know more about the history of District 8 in detail. That is when I was told to contact Gary White, District 8 historian for many years. I had also heard about his wife Sherry, who herself is a Past District Governor from Chicago. (Between us, the little story about them is that they both met at the TI International convention and later got married, and that is how Chicago's loss became District 8's gain! District 8 got Sherry Sala as Sherry White!)

The dinner meeting with Gary and Sherry at their home turned into a very interesting historical expedition. The insight into the depth of the District's evolution, looking at the collection of artifacts and the amount of hard work done by so many people, was a priceless experience. This also affirmed the conviction that this information needed to be documented in the form of a book for District 8's current and future members to recount history now and in distant future."

In that context, a new Toastmaster, Eileen Murphy has proved to be an asset and a testimony of how we connect with each other through our spirit and camaraderie of being a Toastmaster!

As said earlier, I had no idea what I was getting into. But it has been a tremendous experience and a privilege to put this memoire together with the help of Eileen Murphy and District Historian Gary White!
Enjoy the journey of District 8 from 1940's!

Farzana Chohan, DTM
Immediate Past District Director, District 8

> **About: Farzana Chohan**, is a global leader in Management, non-profit and Design. Farzana's life and her experiences has transformed her focus on empowering human leadership. She aspires to use her experiential leadership and academic knowledge to empower humans to live a momentous life.
>
> Farzana's speaking style is described as inspiring with a unique humility that connects with audience at a personal level.
>
> Farzana's credentials include Doctor of management (ABD), Master's and Bachelor's degrees in Architecture. Farzana is a Distinguished Toastmaster (DTM).

Note about Gary White

"For decades, Gary White has been a mentor to all. Gary puts newcomers to experienced Toastmasters at ease. He extends his wealth of experience, knowledge, personableness by taking an interest in each individual to understand their particular challenges or needs. His input was very valuable for me in completing not just my CC manual, but advanced manuals like Humorously Speaking and High Performance Leadership. He agreed to be on my Guidance Committee, a real time commitment.

He supported my Adopt a Highway project and even pick up trash along the highway. That's dedication!

He coached me and others through Contests. When I won, he showed up to support me at the Area and Division levels. He supported my other initiatives like having our club be in the Arnold Parade. I treasure that Gary went above & beyond in so many ways! I will never forget what a difference he made in my life!"

Brook Meadows, Jeffco Challengers Toastmasters

About: Gary White, a Past District Governor of District 8, has a long illustrious association with Toastmasters International. He joined TI in 1974 in Texas (A & M) and never looked back. He moved to District 8 in 1977. Since that time, he has performed leadership roles as Division Governor, Lieutenant Governor and Division Governor. Mr. White has mentored many District Governors including Lorraine Newgent and Dave Smith. He has also been editor of District newsletter (8 Ball) for 3 years. He has served on many committees and has been a co-chair of Regional conference. He has mentored many members and has been a historian since 1988.

Note from Eileen Murphy

First, I want to thank you for reading! This book was the culmination of a lot of passionate work by several different people, and I'm sure I speak for all of us when I say that I take great pride in knowing that other Toastmasters can - hopefully - enjoy the fruits of our labor.

I was the last of many dedicated members of District 8 to be involved in this project. It began several years ago with an idea by Farzana Chohan, DTM, IPDD, who had previously published a book - Spirit of a District 8 Toastmaster - for the district as Public Relations Officer. She wanted to chronicle the impressive and expansive history of District 8, to inspire present and future members with the stories and accomplishments of those who came before us. Longtime District 8 Historian Gary White, DTM, meticulously went over the boxes and boards of magazines, newsletters, programs, and records to provide historical information about the district as much as possible to incorporate in the document.

This left us with a dilemma regarding archival information to what to include in book. Thanks to a few talkative individuals (who shall remain nameless, but they know who they are!), word got around that I had some experience with editing, and soon I, unaware of how this book came to be, was recruited for what I thought would be a simple job of reformatting and proofreading a nearly-finished manuscript. Instead, I got a folder with 224 files and a deadline.

After the initial feeling of what-the-...-have-I-gotten-myself-into wore off, I became very drawn into the project. I was fascinated by the rich history of District 8, the incredible accomplishments of its members, and the outstanding recognition of its clubs by Toastmasters International. I learned that a member of my very own club, which is about to celebrate its 70th anniversary, once served as International President. I gave a speech about him and the history of District 8 to my club, and my evaluator noted how exciting the presentation was, rather than "making us feel like we were in a boring history class."

The world events included in the timeline are my own personal touch to Farzana's idea; I wanted to emphasize the age of the district and how it has adapted in a drastically changing world by giving historical context. District 8 was incorporated one year before a day that shaped the course of history, the attack on Pearl Harbor on December 7, 1941, and is still going strong more than fifteen years after another day that has changed the world forever, September 11, 2001. Of the 77 years of District 8, only 24 of them have been within my lifetime, and through helping to create this book, I feel that I've been gifted with a glimpse into the past – and a personal connection to the legacy of all the Toastmasters who helped to create the group of which I am now proud to be a part.

Eileen Smith-Murphy, CC
VP Public Relations, St. Clair Toastmasters (496)

Acronyms

TM – Toastmasters
DG – District Governor
DTM – Distinguished Toastmasters
IPDG – Immediate Past District Governor
IPDD – Immediate Past District Director
ID – International Director
IP – International President
LGET – lieutenant Governor of Education and Training
LGM – Lieutenant Governor of Marketing
PRO – Public Relations Officer
TI – Toastmasters International
TT – Table Topics

Metamorphosis

www.ingramcontent.com/pod-product-compliance
Lightning Source LLC
Chambersburg PA
CBHW060556200326
41521CB00007B/588